TITANIC

永恒的泰坦尼克

来自深海的真实讲述

汉古艺术馆　美国普利尔展览公司　编

Wuhan Hangu Art Gallery Co., Ltd.　Premier Exhibitions, Inc.

长江出版传媒　湖北美术出版社

序言

这是一个耳熟能详的故事，却又隐藏着太多的神秘。

1912年4月15日凌晨2点20分，泰坦尼克号邮轮沉没在北大西洋距海平面约3800米以下的位置，把辉煌定格在浩瀚海洋的深处。当时船上2228位乘客中，只有700多人逃过此劫，保全了生命。

当泰坦尼克号启程的时候，它宛如一座移动的不夜城，没有人相信它会沉没。因此，这次海难造成的震撼，延续了百年之久。沉没的巨轮，演绎了许多凄美悲凉的故事。人们相信：那些没有到达彼岸的乘客，依然通过沉睡海底的或已经被打捞出水的一件件文物，在无声地叙述他们对自由女神像的翘首盼望以及他们对新大陆生活的无限遐想……

美国普利尔展览公司（拥有RMS泰坦尼克有限公司及从沉船现场打捞文物的所有知识产权）没有片刻遗忘过这艘辉煌的巨轮。1987年，我们就曾以极大的勇气，冒着生命危险，挑战海平面以下3800米的大西洋深海，成为世界第一批潜入到泰坦尼克号沉船遗址的探索者。

从那以后，我们又用了30年的心血，努力去追溯那次永载史册的航行真相，发掘被遗忘在海底的精彩迷人的故事和弥足珍贵的文物。我们利用打捞的文物、乘客的档案、精心制作的视频和音频资料以及展览等多种形式，让全世界走进泰坦尼克的美丽记忆和不朽传奇。

我们非常荣幸和武汉汉古艺术馆合作，为您提供一次探索、沟通和回忆的泰坦尼克之旅。在泰坦尼克的处女航行的乘客中，有爱德华时期的社会各个阶层的人士：世界富豪、巨贾名流、政府官员、中产阶级商人和度假的家庭，以及数百名因经济和宗教压迫首次前往北美的三等舱乘客。无论他们属于哪个社会阶层，在1912年4月15日都经历了同样的命运——快乐的旅行变成噩梦。他们的点点滴滴正是我们今天要讲述的故事，与您分享这些真实的文物和真实故事是我们的荣幸和责任。

美国普利尔展览公司曾耗费数千万美元，于1987年、1993年、1994年、1996年、1998年、2000年、2004年和2010年分八次对泰坦尼克号沉船进行研究和打捞。"鹦鹉螺号"（Nautile）、MIR号潜水艇和远程操作仪器用于打捞文物，并将文物分装到标本篮和吊篮中。潜水器只能容纳三个人：驾驶员、副驾驶和潜水员。每个人都可以通过0.3米厚的舷窗观察深海作业的状况。潜水器需要经过两个半小时才能从海面下潜到泰坦尼克号遗址现场。每一次潜水作业持续约12至15小时，外加2小时上升至水面。我们在泰坦尼克号沉船残骸处打捞出5500多件文物，并对这些文物进行了精心的保护处理。

"泰坦尼克文物精品展览"由美国普利尔展览公司设计，在全球范围内已经有超过2500多万观众参观过这次展览。打捞、保护和展出这些珍贵的文物，为全球观众提供了亲眼目睹沉船实物和用新的视角审视这场悲剧的机会。

　　今天，我们非常荣幸地将这次展览带到中国，邀请中国观众作为泰坦尼克号的乘客，亲身体验处女航之旅的兴奋，以及1912年4月15日那个夜晚的悲剧。我们通过精心挑选的300多件珍贵文物，讲述独一无二且令人难忘的泰坦尼克故事。这些唯一、不可替代的文物承载着船上乘客、船员和邮轮的记忆。在武汉汉古艺术馆展出的每件文物都经过除锈和脱盐处理，在特制的展柜中展出，并被持续监控以及维护，以利于后续的展出和保护。

　　我相信每一位被泰坦尼克号故事感动的人都会对那艘失踪的远洋邮轮有一种特殊的情感。它是一部精彩动人的人生戏剧，涵盖了希腊悲剧的所有经典元素。泰坦尼克号不幸沉入海底迄今已有106年了，但它所承载的精神却未曾离开过我们，爱情、勇敢、担当、牺牲等一系列人类高尚的精神，一直影响并激励着一代又一代的人们。我们的职责就是要让这艘沉没的邮轮从海底升起，继续它没有完成的航行，驶向美好的未来。请您回到1912年的那个夜晚，登上豪华邮轮，走进救生艇，真实地体验历史、感悟今日和明天。

　　如今，你们都是泰坦尼克号的尊贵乘客。请允许我，谨以"永不沉没的泰坦尼克"的第五任"船长"的名义，对您表示欢迎！并对中国武汉汉古艺术馆的卓越工作致以深深的谢意！

鲍道平
美国普利尔展览公司
董事会主席兼行政总裁

PREFACE

Dear Reader,

I want to take you back to 2:20 in the morning on April 15th, 1912, When the RMS *Titanic* sank to her final resting place approximately 2.5 miles beneath the surface of the Atlantic Ocean. Of the 2,228 passengers, more than 1,500 died. No one believed it could happen-not the press, not the government, not the captain and crew and certainly not the passengers. It is a moment in time that has influenced history for more than one hundred years and still has the distinct ability to impact us today.

Premier Exhibitions, Inc. has spent thirty years bringing this story of *Titanic* to life for audiences around the world. Beginning with their first dive to the wreck site in 1987 to their most recent dive in 2010, countless brave and committed men and women have faced enormous challenges to carve out a direction for the future of *Titanic*. Each second of video footage, each artifact recovered and conserved, each passenger profile displayed and each gallery created brings the world one step closer to the memory and legacy of *Titanic*. Premier Exhibitions is truly honored to work with the Wuhan Hangu Art Gallery and offer you the opportunity to explore, connect, remember and immerse yourself in *Titanic's* journey.

Titanic's maiden voyage was a monumental event in history. She was the largest ship sailing the seas in 1912 and reflected every section of Edwardian society. There were captains of industry, government leaders, middle-class businessmen and families on holiday, and there were hundreds upon hundreds of passengers in third-class, many of whom were coming to North America for the first time to escape economic and religious oppression. No matter their class or place in society, they all met with the same fate on April 15th, 1912. They experienced a horrific ending to what began as a joyous journey. Their story is often our story. It is our honor and duty to share these moments with you.

Titanic: The Artifact Exhibition is specially designed by Premier Exhibitions, Inc. and has been viewed by more than 25 million people worldwide. We took exceptional effort and consideration to bring this exclusive opportunity to Wuhan. We uniquely designed this experience for the Wuhan Hangu Art Gallery by allowing you to become a passenger aboard *Titanic's* maiden voyage and experience the excitement and subsequent tragedy of that fateful night in 1912. In addition, we carefully selected hundreds of artifacts for Wuhan, to help tell the unique and memorable stories aboard the Ship. These are one-of-a-kind, irreplaceable artifacts that hold hundreds of memories about each passenger and crew member on board and the Ship itself.

Premier Exhibitions, Inc. has conducted eight research and recovery expeditions to *Titanic's* wreck site in 1987, 1993, 1994, 1996, 1998, 2000, 2004 and 2010 and recovered more than 5,500 artifacts from *Titanic's* debris field Premier is committed to recovering, conserving, and exhibiting artifacts from the *Titanic's* wreck site to help preserve the physical memory of the

Ship and the people who perished in the disaster. Through these activities, people all over the world have the opportunity to see three-dimensional objects that bore witness to the sinking and to gain new insight into the human dimensions of the tragedy.

In order to recover these artifacts, Nautile, MIR submersibles and Remote Operated Vehicles (ROV) are used to scoop and grasp the artifacts, which are then either collected in sampling baskets or placed in lifting baskets. The crew compartment of each submersible accommodates three people: a pilot, a co-pilot, and an observer, who each have a one-foot-thick plastic porthole between themselves and the depths. It takes over two and a half hours to reach the *Titanic* wreck site. Each dive lasts about twelve to fifteen hours with an additional two hours to ascend to the surface.

Each of the artifacts in the Wuhan Hangu Art Gallery underwent conservation following carefully designed processes to remove rust and salt deposits from each object. Artifacts are then ready to be displayed in specially designed cases where they are continuously monitored and maintained so that they can be shown in the exhibition as well as preserved for the future. I encourage you to take yourself back in time to 1912, ask what you would have brought on board and what would you have taken with you in the lifeboats that night. It is truly remarkable for each visitor to be able to relate to these moments of history..I hope these moments continue to influence you long after the exhibition has journeyed on.

I believe each person who is touched by the story of RMS *Titanic* comes away with a special relationship with the lost ocean liner. It is a powerful human drama, with all the classic elements of a Greek tragedy. Almost unimaginable in their variety and complexity, not to mention emotional impact, the stories surrounding the RMS *Titanic*, from its conception, through its well-publicized launch and sailing, to its tragic loss and eventual rediscovery continues to impact and resonate today. We hope you thoroughly enjoy your journey through *Titanic*: The Artifact Exhibition and continue to celebrate the Ship's history and legacy for years to come.

Thank you.

Daoping Bao
Executive Chairman, President & CEO
Premier Exhibitions, Inc.

序言

这是来自深海的讲述。

泰坦尼克号孤独寂静地卧在3800米深的北大西洋海底已经100多年了。这艘当年由英国白星航运公司建造的世界最豪华游轮,以先进的设计理念和极致的奢华体验,被称为"世界工业史上的奇迹"。泰坦尼克号从设计到正式启航,历时3年。1912年4月10日泰坦尼克号从英国南安普顿出发,途径法国瑟堡-奥克特维尔以及爱尔兰昆士敦,驶往美国纽约,开启了她首次也是最后一次航程。1912年4月15日凌晨2时20分,泰坦尼克号不幸撞到冰山,当时船上2228位乘客中,只有705人逃过此劫,获救重生,其余1523名船员和乘客随巨轮沉入海底,成为世界航运史上最惨烈的海难之一。

泰坦尼克号,给世人留下了许多经典的传奇故事和太多未解之谜,虽沉入深海百年却依然吸引着全世界的关注,相信时至今日仍会有很多人为泰坦尼克的故事所感动,某种程度上泰坦尼克可谓"永不沉没"。1985 年,泰坦尼克号沉船位置被成功定位,受到联合国教科文组织保护。美国普利尔展览公司从 1987 年开始,先后八次从大西洋海平面以下 3800 米深的海底陆续打捞出泰坦尼克号沉船上的遗物和沉船残块 5500 多件,这些遗物成为现代史上重要的文化遗存。普利尔展览公司在保护文物的同时,制作了系列泰坦尼克号主题的展览在全球展出,均取得了巨大成功。

2018 年 1 月 11 日,武汉汉古艺术馆有限公司与美国普利尔展览公司在北京签订合作协议,"泰坦尼克文物精品展"今年五月将在武汉展出。此次展览面积达到 2500 多平方米,是"泰坦尼克文物精品展"在世界巡展中面积最大的一次。展览将以在 3800 米深海打捞的真实文物为基础,通过先进的科学技术手段,复原泰坦尼克号重要部分的场景,再现这艘传奇巨轮昔日恢弘的历史篇章。

作为华中地区最大的民营艺术馆,武汉汉古艺术馆肩负着弘扬传统文化、典藏艺术精品、举办特色展览、开展学术研究、普及审美教育、加强国际交流、繁荣文化产业等职责,为大众搭建具有广阔视野和专业标准的公共艺术平台，为武汉及华中地区的文化产业注入新的活力。以艺术馆宽广独特的视觉，引领艺术导向，彰显艺术魅力，打造综合艺术空间，让更多的民众走近艺术，热爱艺术，为武汉的文化产业版图增添光彩。

近年来，随着武汉长江主轴规划的提出，武汉的艺术范围日益浓厚。汉古艺术馆此次不遗余力地引进"泰坦尼克文物精品展"是响应政府号召，彰显企业社会责任及区域文化担当的角色，为大众提供更加丰富与高质量的艺术盛宴，满足大众多元的文化需求，同时也带动武汉地区的文化产业发展，为武汉文化展示增添新的亮点。

泰坦尼克号的故事，承载了太多人的记忆，爱情的伟大，人性的彰显，难以数计的动人情节都将在此次展览中呈现。为配合展览，汉古艺术馆与普利尔展览公司联合编著了《永恒的泰坦尼克——来自深海的真实讲述》一书，以深海打捞出的文物讲述泰坦尼克号的历史背景、人物命运、海难发生、冰海救援、海底发现、深海打捞、文物保护等真实的故事，相信大家在重温历史的同时，也会有很多的启发和感受。

谢小青
武汉汉古艺术馆有限公司董事长

PREFACE

This is a narration from deep sea.

It has been 100 years for Titanic lying in the 3,800m-deep north Atlantic ocean silently. This most luxurious ship in the world made by White Star Line Corporation is known as miracle in the global industrial history with advanced design concept and supreme luxury experience. It took 3 years for Titanic from ship design to official voyage. On 10th April, 1912, Titanic departed from Southampton in Britain through Cherbourg - Octeville in France, and Queenstown in Ireland to New York in America for the first also the last voyage. At 2:20 a.m. 15th April, 1912, Titanic hit iceberg and there were 2,228 passengers onboard among whom only 703 persons spared their lives from this disaster and the other 1,523 sailors and passengers sank into sea with this great ship, which became one of most catastrophic shipwrecks in the world shipping history.

Leaving too many classic legends and unsolved mysteries, Titanic attracted attention from all over the world though it sank into sea over a hundred years. Even now, many people still are moved by Titanic stories. To some extent, Titanic is unsinkable. In 1985, the location of Titanic shipwrecks was successfully isolated, and protected by UNESCO (United Nations Educational, Scientific and Cultural Organization). From 1987, American Premier Exhibitions, Inc. successively salvaged 5,500 items of relics and shipwreck debris of Titanic from 3,800m-depth Atlantic for 8 times in all. These remains have become significant cultural existents in contemporary history. Premier Exhibition, Inc. made series of exhibitions based on the theme of Titanic and exhibits all over the world while protecting these cultural relics. Both the exhibition and the protection achieved great success.

On 11th January, 2018, Wuhan Hangu Art Gallery Co., Ltd. and Premier Exhibition, Inc. signed cooperation agreement in Beijing, and Titanic Antique Exhibition will be held in May in Wuhan. The exhibition area is about 2,500 square meters, which is the largest among those world itinerant exhibitions' so far. This exhibition highlights these antiques salvaged from 3,800m-depth sea and restores some important scenarios of Titanic with advanced science and technology. It reproduced the grand historical chapter of this legendary ship.

As the largest private museum in central China, Wuhan Hangu Art Gallery Co., Ltd. shoulders the responsibility of prompting traditional culture, collecting art pieces, hosting exhibitions, conducting academic researches, popularizing aesthetic education, strengthening international communication, enriching cultural industry, etc. and provides a public art platform with wide view and professional standards for the public, which injects vigor to the cultural industry in Wuhan and even middle China. Hangu Art Gallery embodies a wide and unique perspective, leads art guidance, manifests artistic charm and creates comprehensive art space to let more people get close to art and love art also to add luster to Wuhan cultural industry.

In recent years, artistic atmosphere is increasingly growing as the planning of Wuhan Yangtze spindle is put forward. Wuhan Hangu Art Gallery spares no efforts to bring in Titanic Antique Exhibition in response to Government's call and embodies enterprise's social responsibility and regional culture messenger to provide abundant and high-quality art viewing and satisfy pluralistic cultural needs. Meanwhile, Hangu Art Gallery drives the cultural industry development in Wuhan and is also a move for Wuhan culture exhibition.

The Titanic story not only bears our memories but also embodies great love and humanity and millions of moving plots are shown in this exhibition. Hangu Art Gallery Co., Ltd. and Premier Exhibitions, Inc. co-compiles a book named A real story from deep sea -- Eternal Titanic, narrating true stories of historical background, characters' fate, shipwreck occurrence, ice sea rescue, undersea discovery, deep sea salvage, antique protection. When reviewing the history, we all have a lot of inspiration and feelings.

Xie Xiaoqing
Chairman of the Board
Wuhan Hangu Art Gallery Co., Ltd.

目 录

文 论 1
   泰坦尼克探险 2
   文物的保护 12
   泰坦尼克号上的八名中国乘客 16

图 版 21
   前言 32
   造船与启航 34
   船上生活 44
   冰山和救援 138
   海底和发现 158
   纪念 164

附 录 181
   时间轴线 182
   传奇诞生 184
   船体部件 190
   内部装潢 194
   货物清单 202
   船员信息 204
   问题释疑 210

后 记 214

CONTENTS

1 .... ARTICLE
6 .... *TITANIC* EXPEDITIONS
14 .... CONSERVATION OF THE ARTIFACTS
18 .... EIGHT CHINESE PASSENGERS ON THE *TITANIC*

21 .... CATALOGUE
33 .... Introduction
34 .... Construction and Departure
44 .... Life On Board Galleries
139 .... Iceberg and Rescue
158 .... Seabed and Discovery
164 .... Memory

181 .... APPENDIX
183 .... *Titanic* Timeline
186 .... Birth of *Titanic* Legend
191 .... Parts of the *Titanic*
195 .... Interior Decoration
203 .... *Titanic* Cargo Manifest List
205 .... Crew Members
211 .... Frequently Asked Questions

215 .... POSTSCRIPT

泰坦尼克探险

文物的保护

泰坦尼克号上的八名中国乘客

文 论
ARTICLE

Titanic Expedition

Conservation of the Artifacts

Eight Chinese Passengers on the *Titanic*

泰坦尼克探险

这是震惊世界的海难。1912年4月14日，还有半小时到午夜，号称顶级技术"永不沉没的"泰坦尼克号在加拿大纽芬兰东南600公里处撞上了冰山。两个半小时后，这艘巨大的豪华轮船沉没到海平面以下3800米。船上有2200多名乘客和船员，只有705名生还。一百多年以后，人们不断地讲述着这艘沉船的不幸故事，令世代着迷和不解。沉船数周后便制定了打捞计划，但由于技术原因，计划没有实施，泰坦尼克号被遗忘了几十年。到了20世纪80年代，水下技术取得了巨大进步，最终成功搜寻到泰坦尼克号沉船。

1985年9月1日，在伍兹霍尔海洋研究所（WHOI），由地质学家罗伯特·巴拉德和法国海洋研究利用研究所（IFREMER）的海洋工程师让·路易·米歇尔的带领下，法美联合打捞队在距离官方公布沉船位置的24千米处发现了泰坦尼克号沉船遗骸，拍摄了沉船遗址第一批照片。两年后，美国投资方皇家邮轮泰坦尼克公司，即现在的普利尔展览公司分公司，得到法国海洋探测研究协会许可，首次进行泰坦尼克号沉船遗址搜寻打捞探险。1987年7月，鹦鹉螺号载人潜水器、小型罗宾机器人、纳迪尔科研舰和阿贝耶供给舰驶向泰坦尼克号沉船遗址。1987年7月25日，包括我在内的3名潜水员开始进行1987年泰坦尼克号的首次潜水探险。

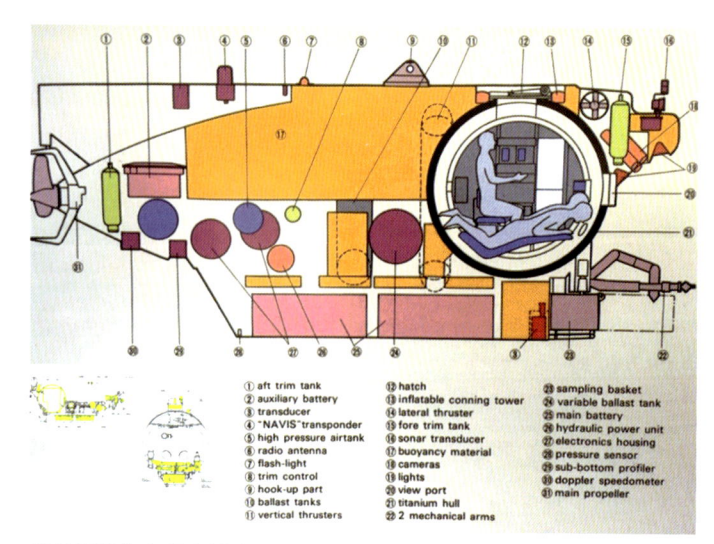

鹦鹉螺号载人潜水器 / Manned submersible Nautile

鹦鹉螺号载人潜水器可以载3人到最深6000米处，空间十分狭小。我们在2.10米的钛球体内工作，周围放满了各种设备，包括声呐、水下电话、视频摄像、显示屏和安全设备。潜水器到达海平面以下3800米需要90分钟。在泰坦尼克遗址处，漆黑一团，外部压力为陆面压力的380倍。在这个深度，所有东西都会受到高压的影响，包括鹦鹉螺号钛球体，它被压力挤压，空间小了几十公升。

抛开科学事实，第一次在沉船遗址看到船甲板和船首时，鹦鹉螺号潜水员都很激动，场面十分壮观。巨大的锚链和闪闪发光的铜绞盘仍在原位，而且保存完好。当我仔细研究沉船残骸时，一股悲喜交加的思绪掠过我的脑海。一方面为众多逝去的生命感到难过，另一方面，面对这艘神话般的沉船，我也感受到一种难以置信的喜悦。

我们很快回到了现实。在这种恶劣的环境下，不能有半点失误。泰坦尼克号沉船是潜水器的潜在危险。在水流的推动下，潜水器会飘浮到沉船危险的一面，撞上沉船。鹦鹉螺号安装了几个安全系统，但是，潜水员意识到这个深度对每个人来讲都有危险。我们想办法监视潜水环境，列出潜水安全预警。第一次潜水时，我们估算了沉船方向和周围的水流速度、潜水系统性能以及鹦鹉螺号和纳迪尔号、海面主船的通讯性能。我勘察了泰坦尼克号残骸区，重要的是标注船首和船尾之间距离为600米。第一次潜水的另一个目的是测试打捞文物的工具。

打捞文物并非易事，在3800米的深度打捞文物是一个挑战。例如，鹦鹉螺号重18000千克，浮力将其调整到海底的中部，以便稳定潜水器的位置。但是，潜水器上没有刹车系统，很难将其停在适合打捞文物的位置。毫无疑问，这对于潜水器操作员来讲十分困难。看见一件文物时，潜水器靠近它，很容易超越目标。由于潜水器不得不使用助推器回到特定文物处，海底沉积物被掀起，干扰了能见度。有时要过20分钟，沉积物才会下沉，视野才会清晰。

鹦鹉螺号有2只由操作员控制的机械手。为了打捞易碎文物，机械手上安装了和空泵相连的吸盘，将像茶杯这样的文物放入潜水器前面手臂之间的打捞篮中。

大型文物被放在从水面放下的"打捞地篮"里。创新是打捞过程中必不可少的。有时打捞特殊文物需要特制工具，比如打捞头等舱图书室的彩色玻璃，在纳迪尔号母船上做了一个与玻璃同样大小的铲，鹦鹉螺号将其插在窗户下方。为了在移动过程中保护玻璃，我们便用木和泡沫在铲和盖之间做了一个夹。确定夹好后，我们小心地将窗户放到巨大的"打捞地篮"里，送到海面。我们的阿贝耶号供给船回收打捞篮子。

我们每天都会即兴创作。很简单，因为没有打捞这个深度沉船残骸区文物的现成工具。他们不得不在晚上或潜水间隔期间自制工具。工具需要更多工程技术，研究制作在探险间隔期间进行。

总之，1987年至2010年，皇家邮轮泰坦尼克美国公司出资组织了8次探险。7次打捞文物，其中载人潜水器潜水136次，鹦鹉螺号潜水112次，另外24次由俄罗斯MIR号潜水器完成，有十多次潜水由远程操作器（ROV）完成，打捞了5849件文物，并在船上完成编号、拍照和保护，然后在岸上特殊实验室里进行处理。值得一提的是，所有打捞文物来自残骸区。我们从未真正进入船内，原因有三个：一是在残骸区有上千件文物；二是很难进入船内；三是出于对在海难中不幸遇难者的尊重，我们不想触动沉船。

文物的尺寸从钻戒到20000千克的船体部件都有。迄今为止，打捞20000千克的文物（我们把它叫做"大家伙"）是所有探险中最大的挑战。我们历时两年，分两次才把这件庞大的钢板打捞出来。1996年，这件"大家伙"第一次露出海面时，刮起了飓风，打捞船上的设备无法上提，"大家伙"又掉到海底。船上的人心都碎了，流下了眼泪。两年后，我们又回到了沉船遗址。我们最最重要的目的就是把飓风中被吹到1000多米以外的"大家伙"打捞上来。8次潜水需要使用6个软体箱。

每个软体箱需要从船箱中加入18000千克柴油，在海平面下3800米温度在1摄氏度的情况下提供3000千克的浮力。3000千克的浮力可以构成较轻的汽油和海水之间的密度差。

为了把软体箱放置到海底，需要将3500千克的重量固定在每个软体箱上。下一步，鹦鹉螺号将每个软体箱移到"大家伙"的附近，再把软体箱一个个固定在"大家伙"上。因为海面强洋流，这个过程十分耗时，但非常必要。一旦软体箱固定了"大家伙"，我们就会释放软体箱的重量，"大家伙"开始上升。它的上升速度很快，只需31分钟。一个半小时以后，"大家伙"被放到供给船的甲板上，长达两年的愿望终于实现了。1996年，当这个"大家伙"第一次掉入水中时，我们潜回海底，在上面挂了个标签，写上"我们会回来的"，这次我们真的做到了。当然，我们是依靠技术、研究和事实生存的科学家，但是潜水至泰坦尼克号远不止这些。在整个过程中，我们的内心充满了强烈的人类原始情感。首次潜水后，我们很快意识到我们不仅探险非同寻常的沉船，打捞具有巨大历史价值的文物，也还原了当时船员们在船上的生活。这些文物不仅是船的记忆，也是船上男人、妇女和儿童的故事。我们怀着对乘客和船员的强烈情感从残骸区打捞文物，解读他们的生活和前往美国的梦想。

但是，打捞文物只是长期艰辛保护工作的开始。文物一上船，就要对其进行保护。文物一旦接触空气，变质过程就会加速。在海上，最好储藏文物的办法是把它放在装有清凉淡水的箱里。一旦上岸，就将其放置在美国和法国的特殊实验室里进行处理和储藏。完成处理后，文物就可以对外展出了。但是，这种处理通常没有终止，每次展览结束，展览项目负责人会对文物进行检查。如果需要，文物会重新回到实验室进行进一步的处理。

软体箱 / Soft tank

在海上，船是一个自治小世界。船员们是一个团队，每个人都有各自的职责，就像一个钟表一样，如果失去一个指针，或者一个指针无法工作，钟就会或慢或快或完全停下来。潜到泰坦尼克号是一次美妙和与众不同的经历，印象深刻，令人难忘。每一次泰坦尼克探险都是不同的冒险，通常受天气的影响。北大西洋海域工作环境十分恶劣，全年大部分时间天气不好，风暴一场接着一场。夏天是探险的"好日子"，低气压的间隔会长些，但是风暴更大。热带低气压随着墨西哥暖流，沿着美国东部沿海经过纽芬兰的泰坦尼克号沉船遗址。在探险期间，一旦风暴袭来，我们就不得不停止潜水，驶到虽然颠簸但却安全的地带。当天气好些时，我们又回到泰坦尼克遗址，再次潜水。

海底的"大家伙"／Big Piece on the ocean floor

几次探险期间，我们看到了来自格陵兰的巨大冰山。今天很容易通过雷达预报和探测冰山。但是，遇到危险仍然十分害怕。几次探险中，冰山飘至离我们仅2千米的地方。接着，墨西哥暖流突然到了，冰山开始快速移动，向东旋转，然后消失。泰坦尼克号沉船过后75年，我们仍然对冰山撞击的后果心有余悸，小心地跟踪它们的踪迹。

另外，除了船员和潜水队，还有其他科学家：造船工程师、金属专家、生物学家、历史学家、考古学家和文物保护专家加入了我们的探险。作为探险成员，他们的职责是研究沉船，检验泰坦尼克号钢铁性能，研究沉船的老化

鹦鹉螺号机械手用吸盘打捞泰坦尼克号玻璃杯／Nautile arm recovering a *Titanic* crystal carafe with the suction cup

状况。生物学家发现导致沉船老化的生物种类。生物会导致沉船金属老化，会"吃"沉船。这种侵蚀过程会加速氧化现象，通过海底水流速度和方向不断变化导致机械老化。在最近的25年间，我们发现沉船变化很大，更多甲板塌陷，救生艇上的洞变大。

潜水器上的人数很简单，两名舵手，然后还有空间留给名人、宇航员、历史学家和泰坦尼克号投资人。标准的潜水要持续8至10小时。因为很多潜水器上的乘客是首次潜水，所以我们要教他们潜水器的安全规则，以及在狭窄空间的生活问题。例如，我们建议他们潜水前一晚尽量少喝水，因为潜水器内没有私密空间和洗手间。

潜水器内的所有电能来自电池。下降到沉船或上升到海面的时间几乎相同。为了节省电能，减少消耗，上升和下降时会关掉推动器。用重力下沉，释放重力上升。潜水器在整个潜水过程中与母船保持通话联系，这对于鹦鹉螺号船员的安全非常重要。显然，在海底没有GPS，鹦鹉螺号使用声控航行系统。20世纪80年代初，这是很先进的深海技术。在过去的三十年里，这一领域取得了长足进步，然而，声控航行还存在困难，因声波在水下无法保持直线。航线取决于水温、盐分和海底地形等问题。今天，大部分潜水器将声控系统和内部导航系统结合使用，这样会大幅度提高潜水定位的准确性。

一旦潜水器定位，有两种方法可以看到沉船。外部勘测可以通过潜水器的3个舷窗进行。泰坦尼克号内部的探测通过鹦鹉螺号安装了的罗宾小型远程操作仪（ROV）完成。罗宾由鹦鹉螺号连线控制，进入沉船内部，鹦鹉螺号船员完成摄影和拍照。为了安全起见，鹦鹉螺号从未真正进入泰坦尼克号沉船。因潜水器的体积太大，而且沉船十分易碎。在潜水期间，我们希望ROV进入沉船更深处，但是，实现这个想法存在着一些问题。有几次罗宾的电缆在沉船内被缠住了，很难解开，潜水器内的船员感到很棘手。幸运的是，我们用电缆把它拉了出来。我们将ROV放进船内，察看沉船内部，最令人震撼的一次是ROV进入一等舱餐厅，我们看见了桌子和墙面装饰遗骸。如果ROV电缆在进入船的核心部位过程中被缠绕住，那我们就不得不启用备用方案。鹦鹉螺号做了最坏的打算，携带了大剪刀，让船员剪掉电缆，脱离潜水器。但是，如果这样，

ROV 将会永远消失。

在探险沉船期间，有时会浮现乘客在船上走动的画面，有时也会想到两名小男孩和他们的父亲，一个法国尼斯家庭的爱的故事，以及泰坦尼克号船上的遇难者和幸存者。Michel Navratil 4 岁时和 2 岁的弟弟以及父亲在英国的南安普敦登上船。他们的护照被偷了，男孩们的父母离婚了，Navratil 先生希望在美国开始新的生活。他还希望这次不辞而别会刺激生活在尼斯的前妻，重新考虑婚姻，跟随家庭前往美国。这位父亲在泰坦尼克号灾难中遇难，男孩们上了救生艇，被送到救下泰坦尼克号所有幸存者的卡帕西亚号船上，驶往纽约。因为护照弄乱了，两名男孩不懂英语，他们在纽约无人认领。报纸将其称为"泰坦尼克号孤儿"。后来，纽约的一位泰坦尼克号幸存者照顾他们。几个星期后，他们的母亲在法国一家报纸上惊讶地认出了孩子，便立即前往纽约领回了孩子。

后来，在几百位泰坦尼克号遇难者中发现了孩子父亲的尸体，飘浮到沉船附近。他被埋在加拿大哈利法克斯墓地，墓上写着被偷护照上的名字。几十年后，两名男孩无法确定是否真的找到了父亲的尸体，最后，他们找到了父亲的墓。在 1996 年泰坦尼克号探险期间，Michel Navratil 第一次前往父亲的墓前吊唁，站在墓前的他已经 88 岁了。他是一名大学哲学退休教师。他后来告诉我们，看到他父亲的墓是他平生收到的最好礼物。

这么多年来，年轻人、老年人，还有孩子们问过我数百个关于泰坦尼克号的问题。令人欣慰的是，他们持续为这个故事着迷，持续关注这一历史事件。我被反复问到的一个问题是有关泰坦尼克号沉船遗址的海洋生物问题。我看到过几种鱼，包括银鲛和三条脚的稀有海底鱼。这种三条"脚"的鱼在海底立起来有 0.2—0.3 米高，泰坦尼克号船内还有白色的螃蟹和海星。

2010 年最后一次探险，我们没有打捞任何文物。作为我们"绘图计划"的一部分，我们决定将泰坦尼克号沉船作为考古遗址，采集高清数据。"绘图计划"采集了皇家邮轮泰坦尼克号和普利尔展览公司七次探险的资料。将最先进的设备用于这个任务，包括两个"深海无人机"，官方称为水下自动装置或 AUV s，我们还使用了远程操作仪（ROV）。这三个设备可以携带高清晰度声呐、摄像机、强光照明和其他高技术设备潜入 6000 米以下。AUVs 涉足泰坦尼克号沉船周围的大部分海域，我们称之为"修剪草坪"，因为它可以抵达东南西北，猎取数千声呐数据和不同角度的照片。ROV 提供船首、船尾和遗址区二维和三维高清图像，这是第一次获得泰坦尼克号遗址复杂的图像，在这张地图上，我们有可能标出文物原来所在的位置以及它和遗址区其他文物的关联。

还有很多有趣的文物需要打捞。今天的技术可以使我们打捞出来很多大型的重型文物，比我们打捞 20000 千克的"大家伙"更容易。我的一个梦想是打捞出泰坦尼克号遗址区 60000 千克的锅炉，我还想取下沉船时连在主发动机上的汽缸。

一百多年后，泰坦尼克号仍然备受关注。最近，我在新英格兰做演讲时，孩子们（多数不满十岁）围绕着我坐在地上聆听，他们的父母和祖父母坐在椅子上听。1912 年的悲剧，每个人都想获取百年旧事的新信息。世界上很少有事件能像泰坦尼克号一样受到关注，触动心灵，引发好奇。普利尔展览公司的宗旨是展出泰坦尼克文物，保护传奇轮船的记忆。我为是公司的一员而感到自豪。

Paul Henry Nargeolet
普利尔展览公司

"大家伙"接近海面 / Big Piece close to the surface

TITANIC EXPEDITIONS

It was a maritime tragedy that shocked the world. On April 14, 1912, a half hour before midnight, the state of the art and reportedly "unsinkable" Ship *Titanic* struck an iceberg 600 km southeast of Newfoundland, Canada. Two and half hours later, the greatest luxury liner of them all sunk at a depth of 3,800 meters. More than 2,200 passengers and crew were on board. Only 705 survived. More than 100 years later, the ill-fated Ship's story continues to resonate, fascinate and mystify generation upon generation. Weeks after the sinking, salvage projects were devised but these plans were not technically realistic. *Titanic* was forgotten for several decades. Then came the 1980s, which brought huge improvements to underwater technology that finally made it possible to successfully search for the *Titanic* wreck.

On September 1, 1985, a French-American team led by geologist Robert Ballard from the Woods Hole Oceanographic Institute (WHOI), and marine engineer Jean-Louis Michel from the French Institute for Research and Exploitation of the Sea, (IFREMER), found the *Titanic* wreck 24 km from the official position where it was said to have sunk. The first pictures of the wreck were taken.

Two years later, a group of American investors, RMS *Titanic*, Inc., now a subsidiary of Premier Exhibitions, chartered IFREMER for the first search and recovery expedition to the *Titanic* wreck site. In July 1987, the manned submersible Nautile along with the small robot Robin, the research vessel Nadir, and the supply vessel Abeille Supporter sailed to the *Titanic* wreck site. On July 25, 1987, three submersible pilots, myself included, conducted the first dive of the 1987 *Titanic* expedition.

The submersible Nautile could dive with three people at the maximum depth of 6000 meters. It was tight quarters for the crew. We worked from inside a 2.10meter Titanium sphere surrounded by a long list of equipment including screen sonar, an underwater telephone, video recorders and screens and safety equipment. It took ninety minutes to reach the bottom of the ocean at 3800 meters. At the *Titanic* site, there was total darkness and the external pressure was 380 times more than the atmospheric pressure on the surface. At this depth, everything was significantly affected by the intensely high pressure, including the Nautile titanium sphere which was squeezed by the pressure and lost a volume of a few dozen liters.

Setting scientific facts aside, the Nautile crew was overwhelmed with emotion when we arrived at the wreck site and viewed for the first time, the deck of the bow section. It was a magnificent sight. The large anchor chains and shining bronze winches were still in place and in remarkably good shape. A mixture of bittersweet thoughts ran through my head as I studied the details of the wreck. On the one hand, I felt sadness thinking about all the lives lost. On the other hand, I was also sensing incredible joy to be face to face with this mythical wreck.

Very quickly, we returned to reality. In this very hostile environment, there is no room for error. The *Titanic* wreck was a potential trap for a submersible. Pushed by the currents the submersible could drift over a dangerous part of the wreck and get stuck there. Nautile had several safety systems but the submersible

软体箱下沉 /
Descent weight for soft tank

crew

realized that at this depth it was a matter of every man for himself. Knowing the potential dangers involved with the dive, we went out of our way to monitor the dive conditions and list warnings to make the dives safe. During the first dive, we evaluated the direction and speed of the current around the wreck, the efficiency of the navigation system and the quality of communications between the Nautile and the Nadir, the mother ship on the surface. We also had to make a survey of the *Titanic* debris field. It is important to note that the bow and the stern are located 600 meters from each other. Another goal of this first dive was to test tools made for recovering artifacts.

Recovering artifacts is not an easy job. And at the tremendous depth of 3.8 km, the assignment can prove to be especially challenging. For example, the Nautile weighs 18000kg. Its buoyancy is adjusted to neutral at the bottom of the sea in order to stabilize the sub's position. But there are no brakes on the sub, making it difficult to stop at the right position for recovering artifacts. This is arguably the most difficult task for a sub pilot. When an artifact is seen, and the sub approaches it, it's very easy to overshoot the mark. Because the sub has to use its propellers to return to that particular artifact, sediment on the ocean floor is stirred up, disturbing the visibility. Sometimes we waited twenty minutes for the sediment to settle and the visibility to clear.

The Nautile had two mechanical arms controlled by the pilot. To recover fragile artifacts, the jaw of the arm was equipped with a small suction cup connected to a vacuum pump. An artifact such as a teacup was dropped into a basket between the arms in front of the submersible.

The larger artifacts were dropped into a "field basket" placed in the debris field from the surface. Creativity was a very necessary part of the process. Sometimes special tools had to be made to recover specific artifacts. This was the case, for example, for recovering a stained-glass window from the First-Class Library. A shovel the size of the stained glass was built on the mother ship Nadir and slipped under the window by the Nautile. To protect this stained-glass window even more during the move, it was sandwiched in between the shovel and a cover made of wood and foam. After closing and securing what we called the "wallet," we carefully lowered the window into a jumbo-sized field basket and sent it to the surface. Our supply boat Abeille Supporter recovered the basket.

We leaned on improvised everyday. Quite simply, there were no ready-made tools to recover artifacts in a debris field of a wreck at this depth. They had to be created, either during the night or in between the dives. Tools requiring more engineering and study were built ashore in between the expeditions.

In total, the American company RMS *Titanic*, Inc. financed and organized eight expeditions from 1987 to 2010. Seven of those expeditions recovered artifacts. This included 136 dives in manned submersibles. Nautile was used for 112 of those dives. Twenty-four additional dives were completed by the two Russian submersibles Mirs. Then there were ten more unmanned dives using a Remotely Operated Vehicle (ROV). We brought up 5,849 artifacts. They were indexed, photographed and preserved on board the ship, then treated on land at specialized laboratories. It is important to note that all artifacts were recovered only from the debris field. We never actually entered the Ship for three reasons: (1) There were thousands of artifacts in the debris field, (2) it was very difficult to enter the Ship (3) we didn't want to touch the Ship, out of respect for the people who lost their lives in the tragedy.

装满柴油的软体箱 /
Soft tank full of diesel fuel

The size of the artifacts ranged from a diamond ring to

a 20000kg section of the *Titanic* hull. The recovery operation for that huge 20000kg artifact, named the "Big Piece," was, by far, the biggest challenge of all the expeditions.

Bringing this mammoth chunk of steel to the surface took not one but two expeditions, occurring over a span of two years. In 1996, just as the Big Piece was being raised out of the ocean for the first time, hurricane force winds kicked up and the equipment from the recovery ship was not adapted to handle the lifting. The Big Piece fell back down to the bottom of the sea and there was heartbreak and tears on board the ship. Two years later, we returned to the wreck site. Our most important goal was to recover the Big Piece, which by now had drifted ten miles away during the storm. Eight dives were needed using six soft tanks.

Each soft tank contained 18000kg of diesel fuel from the ship tanks and provided three tons of buoyancy at 3800 meters with the sea temperature at 1 degree Celsius. The 3000kg buoyancy was created utilizing the difference of density between the much lighter gas oil and the seawater.

3500kg of weights had to be fastened to each soft tank in order to send them to the bottom of the ocean. The next step in the process was for the Nautile to move each soft tank near the Big Piece and connect the tanks, one by one, to the Big Piece. It was a very time- consuming process and yet very necessary because of the strong surface current. Once the soft tanks were attached to the Big Piece, we released the descent weight for each tank and the Big Piece began to rise. It was a quick ascent, lasting only 31 minutes. An hour and a half later, the Big Piece was on the deck of the supply vessel and a two-year-old promise had been came true. The first time the Big Piece dropped back into the sea in 1996 we dove back down and affixed a plaque to it. The plaque said, "We will come back." And we did.

Yes, of course, we were scientists who lived our lives based on technology, research and facts. But diving on the *Titanic* was much more than that. Strong currents of raw human emotion ran through our hearts and minds during the entire project. Quickly, after the first dives, we realized that we were not only exploring an extraordinary wreck and recovering artifacts of great historical value, but we were resurrecting the lives that had existed on the Ship. These artifacts not only salvaged the memory of a great Ship but the stories of the men, women and children on board. In the debris field, as we collected artifacts, we felt a strong emotional connection to both the passengers and crew. We learned about their lives and their dreams going to America as we plucked objects from the sediment.

But recovering artifacts was just the beginning of a long painstaking process to preserve them for the ages. The moment the artifacts were brought to the ship, it was a race against time to preserve them. Once they were in contact with the air, the deterioration process accelerated. At sea, the best way to store the artifacts was to submerge them in tanks of cold fresh water. Once ashore, they were treated and restored at specialized laboratories, both in the U.S. and France. Only after the conservation process was completed could the artifacts be exhibited to the public. But this treatment is often not final. At the end of each exhibition, the artifacts are checked by our curators. If an additional treatment is needed they go back to the laboratory.

At sea, a ship is a small autonomous world. The crew functions as a team, everyone is necessary. Like a clock, if a piece is missing or does not work, the clock slows down, speeds up or stops altogether. Diving on the *Titanic* was a fantastic and unique experience, full of powerful, unforgettable memories. Each *Titanic* expedition had its own, very individualized set of adventures, often shaped by the weather. The North Atlantic is an extremely difficult area to work in. The weather is bad a large part of the year and one storm is followed by the next. The "good time" for the expeditions in summertime, the space between depressions is longer, however, the storms are stronger. These tropical depressions follow the Gulf Stream along the east coast of the United States and then pass over the *Titanic* wreck off of Newfoundland. During the expeditions, when a storm was coming to us, we had to stop the dives, and sail away at a safe distance though things were often still bumpy. When the weather was better we were able to come back to the *Titanic* site and dive again.

Several times during the expeditions, we saw huge icebergs coming from Greenland. Today they are easily reported and detected by radar. But we are still very afraid of dangerous. During some of our expeditions, icebergs were drifting less than two kilometers away from us. Then suddenly, entering the Gulf Steam, they began to move faster, whirled off to the east and disappeared. More than three quarters of a century after the *Titanic* tragedy, there we were, still wary of the deadly consequences of icebergs and carefully tracking their course.

Beside the crews of the ships and the submarine teams, we had other scientists joining us on the expeditions: naval architects, metal specialists, biologists, historians, archeologists and conservators. As members of the expedition, their duty was to study the different phases of the sinking, to check the quality of steel and iron used for *Titanic* and to study the deterioration of the wreck. The biologists on the expedition found a species of bacteria which was one of the causes of the deterioration of the Ship. This bacterium was consuming particles of steel and iron on the wreck for its metabolism, as in, the bacteria "ate" the wreck. This destructive process came in addition to the oxidation phenomena, and to the mechanical deterioration done by the bottom current changing continuously in speed and direction. Over twenty-five years, we have seen significant changes in the wreck. The decks are collapsing and big holes are growing on the lifeboat deck.

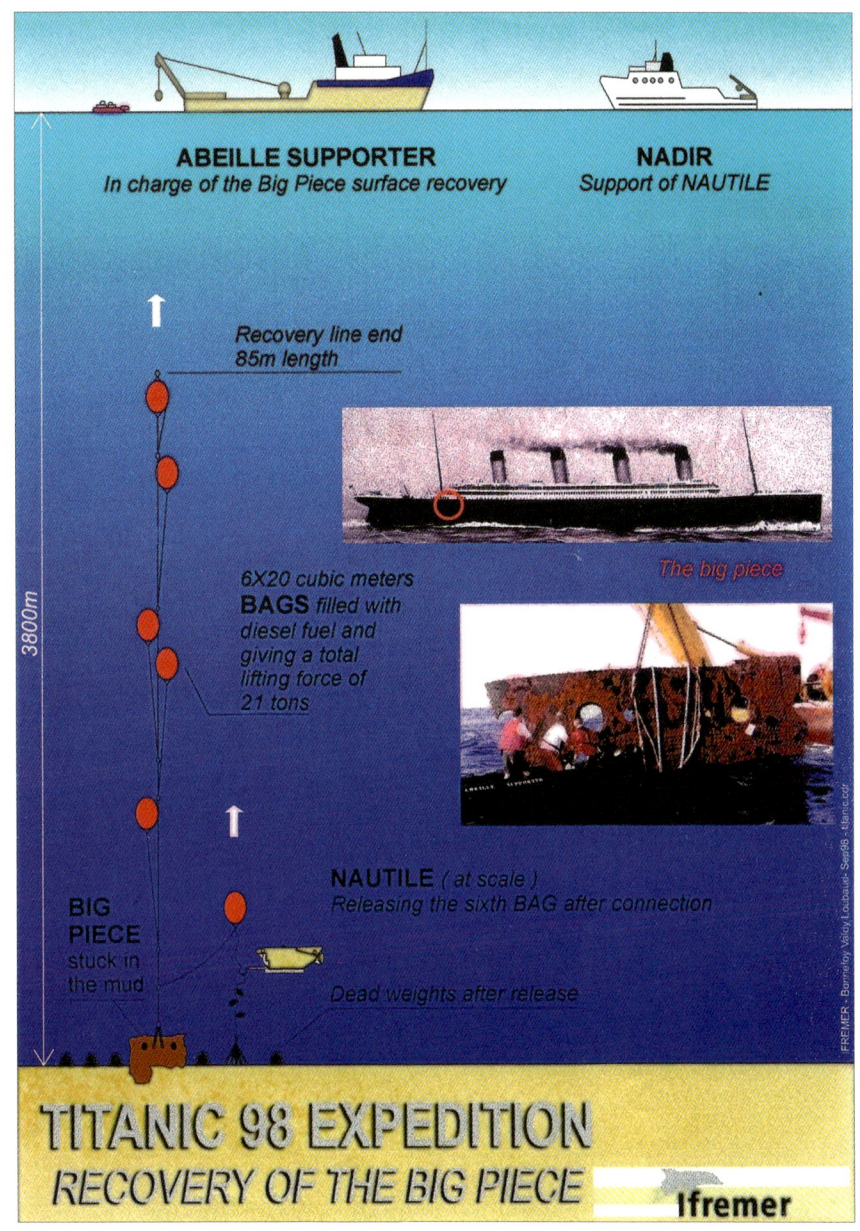

"大家伙"的打捞操作 / Big Piece recovery operation

The numbers were simple aboard the sub. Two pilots were always required. Then there was the coveted third space, available to celebrities, astronauts, historians and *Titanic* investors. A typical dive lasted between eight and ten hours. For many sub passengers, it was their first dive, so we had to teach them submersible safety rules as well as the life issues involved with a small sphere. We advised them, for example, to drink as little as possible the night before their dive, because of the lack of privacy and the absence of a bathroom in the submersible.

9

All the energy available on board the submarine was supplied by battery packs. It took almost the same time to descend to the wreck or ascend to surface. To save the life of the batteries and minimize electric consumption, the propellers were turned off for both ascent and descent. Gravity did the job, assisted by the use of weights for the descent and the release of weights for the ascent. The submarine remained in voice contact with the mother ship during the entire dive. This was absolutely essential for the security of the Nautile crew. Obviously, there was no GPS at the bottom of the ocean. The Nautile used an acoustic navigation system, which in the early 1980s, was a new technical advancement for deep water. In the past thirty years, tremendous progress has been made in this area, however, acoustic navigation remains a difficult issue. The problem is that sound waves don't travel in a straight line underwater. Their path depends on a few things, including water temperature, salinity and the shape of the ocean bottom. Today most submersibles mix this acoustic system with an inertial navigation system, which dramatically increases the accuracy of the sub position.

Once we positioned the sub, there were a couple of ways to look at the wreck. The survey of the exterior was done through the three portholes of the submersible. For the *Titanic* interior exploration, the Nautile was equipped with Robin, a small Remotely Operated Vehicle (ROV). The Robin was wire-guided from the Nautile and was able to be driven through small openings inside the wreck. Video and photos were recorded by the Nautile crew. For safety reasons, the Nautile was never allowed to actually go inside the *Titanic* wreck. The sub's dimensions were too big and the wreck was too fragile. During the dives, we always expected to go farther and penetrate deeper into the wreck using the ROV. However, there were problems with this idea. Several times, Robin's cable became tangled inside the wreck. It was not always easy to free it up, giving the sub's crew a hard time. Fortunately, we had a happy ending with the cable. We were able to release it and explore the wreck's interior. One of the most thrilling moments was when the ROV was inside the First-Class Dining Room, showing us the remains of the tables and the wall decorations. Had the cable for the ROV become hopelessly tangled on its way to the heart of the ship, we had a fallback plan. In the worst case, the Nautile was equipped with a double pyrotechnic shear that would allow the crew to cut the cable and free the submersible, but in this case, Robin(ROV) would be lost forever.

During the exploration of the wreck, we sometimes pictured passengers moving about the Ship. Two small boys and their father came to mind, a French family from Nice with an incredible story of love, loss and survival aboard the *Titanic*. Michel Navratil was four-years-old when he boarded the Ship with his two-year-old brother and father in Southampton, England. The passports had been stolen. The boys' parents had divorced and Mr. Navratil's hope was to start a new life in America. He also hoped this shocking move would inspire his ex-wife, who was living in Nice, to reconsider the marriage and follow the

在泰坦尼克号船首位置的罗宾小型远程操作仪 /
Remotely Operative Vehicle ROBIN on the *Titanic* Bow

family to the United States. The father did not survive the *Titanic* tragedy. His boys, meanwhile, were put in a lifeboat and sailed to New York aboard the passenger ship Carpathia, which saved all the *Titanic* survivors. Because of the passport mix-up and the fact that the boys did not speak English, they became a mystery in New York. Newspapers dubbed them "The *Titanic* Orphans." A *Titanic* survivor from New York City took care of the boys. Weeks later, their stunned mother recognized the faces of her children in a French newspaper. She immediately sailed to New York to retrieve them. The father's body was found later, among a few hundred *Titanic* victims, drifting in the vicinity of the sinking. He was buried in the Halifax cemetery in Canada, his grave bearing the name on the stolen passport. For decades, the boys wondered if their father's body had ever been found but finally they learned the location of his grave. During the 1996 *Titanic* expedition, Michel Navratil was able to pray at his father's grave for the first time in his life. At that time, he was 88 years old. He's a retired university philosophy teacher overcome with emotion. He later told us, seeing his father's grave was the best gift he ever received.

I've been asked hundreds of questions about the *Titanic* over the years, questions posed from both the young and old; new generations of children. By the way, they continue to be fascinated by this story and I am amazed at their interest in a century-old event. One of the questions I am frequently asked is about the marine life around the *Titanic* wreck site. I saw several kinds of fish including ratfish and the Benthos fish, a rare species that appears to be standing on a tripod. These three "legs" elevate the fish from the bottom of the ocean by 20-30 cm. The *Titanic* was also inhabited by white crabs and starfish.

During our last expedition in 2010 we did not recover artifacts. As a part of our "mapping project", we decided to collect very high-quality data and to treat the *Titanic* wreck as an archaeological site. The "Mapping Project" assembled all the data collected from the first seven expeditions by RMS *Titanic* and Premier Exhibitions. State of the art equipment was used for this assignment including two "deep sea drones," officially called Autonomous Underwater Vehicles or AUV's. We also used a Remotely Operated Vehicle, (ROV). All three of these vehicles were capable of diving at 6000 meters and carrying high definition sonars, video cameras, powerful lights and other high-tech equipment. The AUVs crisscrossed a large area around the *Titanic* wreck. We fondly called this "mowing the lawn," as the AUV ran north to south and east to west, taking thousands of sonar and optical pictures at different altitudes. The ROV was providing 2 and 3-D film in high definition, of the bow and the stern of the wreck and the debris field in between. It was the first comprehensive map of the *Titanic* wreck site ever made and the high definition gave us sensational results. On this map, it was possible to plot all the artifacts recovered at their original location and to relate them to artifacts still lying in the debris field.

And there are still many interesting artifacts to recover. Today's technology allows us to lift up very large and heavy artifacts with far more ease than the drama we faced with the 20000kg Big Piece. One of my dreams is to recover one of the 60000kg boilers lying on the *Titanic* debris field. I'd also like to retrieve one of the cylinders, which detached from the main engine during the sinking.

Over one hundred years later, *Titanic* continues to captivate the public. At a recent lecture in New England, small children, all of them under the age of ten, gathered around me on the floor, as their parents and grandparents listened from their chairs in the crowded room, everyone wondering and wishing for new facts on a long-ago tragedy from 1912. Few events in the world have held the public's attention, touched hearts and challenged curiosities like the *Titanic*. I'm very proud to be a part of Premier Exhibitions, whose main goal is to exhibit *Titanic* artifacts and preserve the memory of this legendary Ship for generations to come.

Paul Henry Nargeolet
Premier Exhibition,Inc

文物的保护

　　1994 年，美国联邦法院裁决皇家邮轮泰坦尼克公司 (RMS *Titanic*, Inc.) 独家拥有皇家邮轮泰坦尼克号沉船残骸的打捞权。该裁决于 1996 年被再次确认。此权利中也包括拥有沉船遗址文物的独家打捞权。打捞泰坦尼克文物的探险活动由皇家邮轮泰坦尼克公司 (RMS *Titanic*, Inc.)、法国海洋研究所和莫斯科希尔绍夫（P.P.Shirshov）海洋研究所共同合作完成。在 1987 年、1993 年、1994 年、1996 年、1998 年、2000 年和 2004 年期间先后进行了七次研究性打捞，皇家邮轮泰坦尼克公司打捞文物共计 5500 多件，其文物范围从一个巨大的、重达 15.422 千克的船体外壳部分，到一个微小的、其直径仅有 0.127 米的儿童玩具——大理石球。皇家邮轮泰坦尼克公司 (RMS *Titanic*, Inc.) 还保留了有关文物打捞和文物保护方面的详尽数据档案和遗址照片资料。2010 年第八次研究性探险又确立了遗址区的边界，记录了沉船的二维图和三维图，并绘制了第一张遗址照片地图。

　　皇家邮轮泰坦尼克公司 (RMS *Titanic*, Inc.) 的文物保护计划旨在阻止这些文物的状况恶化，对几十年来受到海底有害物质侵蚀的文物进行保护，以便在对外展出时，把它们最原始的面貌呈现给观众。在打捞泰坦尼克号文物之前，人们对如何保护从 3800 米深的海底打捞出的文物缺乏经验，几乎没有任何专业的深海文物保护资料可以借鉴。这些文物处于氧气很少，没有光的状况，而且每平方厘米的压力超过了 380 公斤。因此，文物保护工作者需要寻找一套新的方法来处理和保护这些独一无二的文物。

　　随着时间的推移，人造物品会被盐和酸腐蚀，被沉积物和细菌侵蚀，甚至船体本身也会慢慢地被吃铁微生物损坏而最终在海底倒塌，沉船遗址中没有打捞上来的文物最终将会消失。皇家邮轮泰坦尼克公司正在致力于打捞、保护和展出泰坦尼克号沉船遗址的文物，保留沉船和在灾难中遇难者的实物记忆。通过这些工作，让全世界有机会看到打捞的文物，对悲剧中的人性有一个新的认识。

　　一旦决定打捞某一件文物，就需要全面了解它的处理方法、如何维护和永久性的保护措施。保护泰坦尼克号文物需要一个由文物保护工作者、展览项目负责人、登记员、考古学家、历史学家和其他专家组成的合作团队，以便提供从打捞到收藏的持续保护。严格遵照这些规定，皇家邮轮泰坦尼克公司 (RMS *Titanic*,Inc.)/ 普利尔公司可以在尊重历史和皇家邮轮泰坦尼克传奇的同时，安全地与公众分享这些独一无二的文物。

　　从泰坦尼克号打捞上来的文物不仅包括金属、陶瓷、玻璃、纺织品、纸质品、皮制品，以及诸如橄榄、坚果和香皂这些实用品，还包括了从船运行所需的工具和设备到乘客和船员的个人物品。这些文物在船体下沉时散落在海底，不只遭受到物理损坏，还要经历来自盐水、气体、酸性土壤与电化学反应的化学侵蚀，以及来自锈蚀和船蛆生物化学的侵害。

每件物品打捞上来后，都需要立即对其进行稳定性处理，以防止因环境的突然改变而进一步加剧它们的分解。在海面对每件文物的稳定性初步控制后，文物保护工作者首先要对每件文物进行拍照、测量和评估，并逐一建立识别号码和项目编号，以及打捞时间记录，然后将这些信息输入数据库。当文物从盐水里打捞出来时，需要放在装有淡水的泡沫箱内，用软刷清洗。最后，这些文物会被放在有保湿泡沫内衬的箱子里，贴上标签，以便于安全地送至陆地实验室。一旦进入实验室，就要去掉每件文物表层的盐渍，这个过程叫脱盐处理。每件文物必须进行脱盐处理，否则文物状况会持续恶化。

泰坦尼克号文物由大量不同的材质组成，一旦上岸，就需要纸质、纺织、木制、金属、陶瓷和皮革制品的专业保护团队介入。所有的保护技术都与文物相关，无论如何，大多数文物收藏时，都需要经过脱盐、干燥、保护和修复等诸多环节。在经过 6 个月至 2 年的脱盐处理后，可以根据每件文物的材质进行处理收藏。玻璃、瓷器等材质相对简单，而复杂文物，如怀表、双筒望远镜则需要多种不同的处理方法。

金属物品通常放在脱盐缸内经过脱盐清洗，并进行第一步的电解，以去掉物品表面上的负离子和盐。目前电解也用于纸、皮革和木制品脱盐。之后，还要用化学药剂和杀菌剂进一步处理，以去除这些金属物品上的腐蚀物和真菌。纸质品首先需要经过冰冻干燥处理除去水分，然后用专用吸尘器和工具除去污渍和残留物。皮革制品用浸泡方法或向物品内注入一种水溶性蜡，填充到之前被水分和碎屑充满的空隙中。

经过保护处理后，文物被放在温度、相对湿度、光线可控的专用展柜中，以免文物受到这三种因素的伤害。展出文物在经过保护处理后，被持续监控和维护，以确保展览的展示和未来的收藏。

遗憾的是，没有保护船体本身的保护技术，船体正在慢慢地被一种食铁细菌所吞噬。科学家们预言泰坦尼克号船体将在 40 至 90 年内倒塌。尽管无法确定沉船的未来，但在船消失后，泰坦尼克号沉船遗址的文物会长久保留。这些文物，记载了传奇般的航行、提示了生命的脆弱、见证了在无法形容的悲剧面前，人类的精神力量。

Alexandra Klingelhofer
普利尔展览公司

CONSERVATION OF THE ARTIFACTS

RMS *Titanic*, Inc. was granted salvor-in-possession rights to the wreck of RMS *Titanic* by a United States Federal Court order in 1994. That order was reconfirmed in 1996. This award includes the exclusive rights to recover artifacts from the wreck site. Expeditions to recover *Titanic* artifacts have been a collaborative effort between RMS *Titanic*, Inc.; The French Oceanographic Institute; and the Moscow-based P.P. Shirshov Institute of Oceanology. During seven research and recovery expeditions conducted in 1987, 1993, 1994, 1996, 1998, 2000 and 2004, RMS *Titanic*, Inc. has recovered over 5,500 artifacts, ranging from a massive 15,422 kg portion of the hull to a delicate child's marble measuring only 0.127m in diameter. RMS *Titanic*, Inc. maintains a comprehensive digital archive of these recovered and conserved artifacts as well as photographic data from the site. An eighth research expedition in 2010 established the perimeter of the wreck site, recorded the Ship in 2DHD and 3DHD imagery, providing the first ever photographic map of the site.

The goal of RMS *Titanic*, Inc.'s artifact conservation program is to stop deterioration while allowing recovered objects to be exhibited while bearing witness to the horrific sinking and exposure to hostile elements during their decades on the ocean floor. Before the recovery of *Titanic's* artifacts, there was little expertise in conserving materials retrieved from a deep-sea environment. At a depth of 3,800 (meters) kilometers, there is little oxygen, no light, and pressure greater than 380 kg per square centimeter (380kg/cm2). Conservators had to develop new methodologies to treat and preserve these unique artifacts.

Over time, man-made objects will be corroded by salt and acids, abraded by sediments, and consumed by bacteria. Even the Ship itself is slowly being destroyed by iron-eating microorganisms and will one day collapse on the ocean floor. Artifacts that are not recovered from the wreck site will eventually be lost. RMS *Titanic*, Inc. (RMST) is committed to recovering, conserving, and exhibiting artifacts from *Titanic's* wreck site to help preserve the physical memory of the Ship and the people who perished in the disaster. Through these activities, people all over the world have the opportunity to see recovered objects and to gain new insights into the human dimensions of the tragedy.

Once a decision is made to recover an artifact, there is full knowledge of the commitment to treatment, care and preservation in perpetuity. Preserving *Titanic* artifacts requires a collaborative team of conservators, curators, registrars, archaeologists, historians, and other experts to provide continual care and maintenance of the collection from the moment of recovery onward. By strictly following these procedures, RMST/Premier can safely share these unique artifacts with the public, while respecting their historical context and the RMS *Titanic* legacy.

Artifacts recovered from *Titanic* include metals, ceramics, glass, and, surprisingly, textiles, papers, leather, and materials such as olives, nuts, and soap. They range from tools and equipment needed to run the Ship to personal items of passengers and crew. During the sinking and exposure on the ocean floor, these artifacts were subject to physical damage; chemical deterioration from salt water, gases, acidic soils, and electrochemical reactions; and biochemical attack from rusticles and shipworms.

Immediately upon retrieval, each object is stabilized to prevent further degradation due to its sudden change of environment. In the initial stabilization at sea, conservators photograph, measure, and assess the condition of each artifact. They then enter this information into a database and assign each artifact an identifying accession number, which provides the expedition year and item number. When recovered from salt water, artifacts are cleaned with a soft brush and placed in foam-lined tubs of fresh water. Finally, the artifacts are placed in bins lined with moist foam and tagged for secure transit to conservation laboratories on land. Once received at the conservation laboratory, contaminating surface salts are removed from each artifact. This process is called desalination and must be applied to each artifact or deterioration will continue.

Titanic's artifacts are comprised of a vast array of materials and, once on land, require a team of conservators who specialize in papers, textiles, woods, metals, ceramics, and leathers. All conservation techniques are artifact-specific, however, desalination, drying, protection, and maintenance are all employed while conserving most materials in the collection. After a desalination period of six months to two years, artifacts can be conserved using treatments that are compatible with each artifact's construction materials. Glass, hard-fired ceramics, and similar materials are relatively straightforward, while treatment of complex artifacts such as pocket watches or binoculars may require several different treatments.

Metal objects are often placed in a desalination bath and undergo the first steps of electrolysis, a process that removes negative ions and salt from the artifact. Electrolysis is now being used to remove salts from paper, leather, and wood as well. These materials also receive treatments of chemical agents and fungicides that remove other corrosion products and fungus from them. Artifacts made of paper are first freeze-dried to remove water and are then cleaned with specialized vacuums and hand tools to remove dirt and debris. Leather artifacts are soaked or injected with a water-soluble wax which replaces voids previously filled by water and debris.

Once conserved, artifacts are displayed in specially designed cases where temperature, relative humidity and light levels can be controlled, protecting the artifacts from these three agents of deterioration. The artifacts displayed have been conserved and are continuously monitored and maintained so that they can be shown in the exhibition as well as being preserved for the future.

Unfortunately, there are no conservation techniques to preserve the Ship itself, which is slowly being consumed by iron-eating bacteria. Scientists predict this process will cause *Titanic* to collapse on itself in forty to ninety years. Despite the uncertain future of the wreck, *Titanic's* recovered artifacts will remain long after the Ship is gone as a reminder of the legendary liner, life's fragility, and the power of the human spirit to face unspeakable tragedy.

Alexandra Klingelhofer
Premier Exhibitions, Inc

泰坦尼克号上的八名中国乘客

泰坦尼克号的乘客名单中，记录着八位中国人的名字：Fang Lang、Lee Bing、Ali Lam、Chang Chip、Choong Foo、Len Lam、Ling Hee 和 Lee Ling。有关这八个中国人的英文名字拼法，一百年来，国外媒体一直存在着争议。

美国国家档案馆里，也可以查询到其中几个人的繁体字中文签名，例如：钟捷、李柄、炳新……这八个人中，最小的 24 岁，最大的 37 岁。除 Lee Bing 已婚外，其他人都是单身。Ali Lam 和 len Lam 是中国籍的广东人。其他六人是持有英国护照的香港人，他们在外国轮船上当锅炉工。

需要特别说明的是，他们只是泰坦尼克号船上的普通乘客。他们登上泰坦尼克号，是因为当时英国的煤炭工人罢工而丧失了原有的工作，他们又在一家名为唐纳德的船运公司找到了新的工作机会，便一起赶到英国的南安普敦，计划从那里乘坐泰坦尼克号前往纽约。待抵达纽约后，他们将改搭途经纽约的 Annetta 号轮船继续前往古巴，去唐纳德船运公司工作。他们仍然需要经过美国移民局批准，但依据当时美国的排华法案，中国人不允许进入美国。

唐纳德船运公司预先为他们垫付了集体船票，这八名中国劳工共同使用一张船票，号码为 160，票价为 59 英镑 9 先令 11 便士，船舱等级为三等舱。

当时西方社会森严的等级制度，也体现在泰坦尼克号的船舱级别上。三等舱的乘客在船上受到的另一个被歧视的限制是：他们只能待在三等舱中，不允许与船上的其他乘客社交来往。他们不可以在船尾甲板自由出入，也不能去上层甲板观光。三等舱的乘客大部分都是来自欧洲各地的移民，他们准备去到美国开辟新生活。

三等舱所提供的基本设施对于普通乘客来说，已经是一种享受！泰坦尼克号三等舱的居住条件还是比较舒适的，有宽敞的公共休息室和公共吸烟室，有两个公共的澡盆，分为男用和女用。睡觉的房间配有弹簧床垫、枕头、毯子，房间里也配备了洗漱池、小衣柜和床头取暖器等。三等舱餐厅的食物虽然简单，但品种丰富，有燕麦片、牛奶、面包、熏鲱鱼、牛排和水果等。这八名中国人一定不会想到，在他们刚刚开始放松心情娱乐休息的时候，一场海难将这一切无情地结束了！

在海难发生的时候，Fang Lang 趴在一块木板上，是 14 号救生艇指挥官罗威救上来的最后一位乘客。当时他已经四肢冻僵，奄奄一息，经过救生艇上几位乘客按摩，他几乎在 5 分钟之内就恢复了体力。当他发现身边的一位船员因过度疲劳而快要晕倒时，他接过船桨，用力划起船来。指挥官罗威称赞他"看起来像个英雄！"，他以自己的实际行动很快赢得了救生艇上所有乘客的尊重。

当面临船舱进水，船体倾斜时，名为 Choog Foo 的中国人上了 13 号救生艇。Lee Bing、Ali Lam、Chang Chip、Len Lam、Ling Hee 和 Lee Ling 也分别上了不同的救生艇。也许他们比较了解救生艇的内部构造，他们都在救生艇的底层寻找到了他们认为可求生的最佳位置。但选择安身在救生艇的板条之下的 Len lam 和 Lee Ling 却难逃一死。究其死亡原因，一种认为是坐在救生艇上面的乘客体重过重，而将这两名中国人活活压死在底层的板条下。但事实上，他们可能死于体温过低。

1912 年 4 月 15 日凌晨 2 点 40 分，赶来救援的 Carpathia 号，将泰坦尼克号上的 705 名幸存者送至纽约。在纽约港，泰坦尼克号上的头等舱和二等舱的乘客，都办理了入境美国的手续而获准下船。而三等舱的乘客则继续乘坐 Carpathia 号到了埃利斯岛。在那里，所有乘客都被允许下船，只有这六名中国人受到当时美国排华法案的限制而不准进入美国被滞留在 Carpathia 号船上，第二天就被直接带到 Annetta 号船上，随船驶向古巴，继续为唐纳德船运公司打工。

海难之后，幸存的六名中国人，除 Fang Lang 外，上岸后都遭到质疑，美国媒体以不可思议的口气对这几名求生的中国人进行了报道。中国上海《申报》也有相关报道。

1912 年 4 月 17 日，美国对华协会特别理事亨利·福特试图为泰坦尼克号上的这些中国人的行为做出辩解，他致辞《纽约时报》："在中国，救人顺序是以男人为先，儿童次之，妇女最后。这是因为男人在中国的地位很高，孩子失去亲人，可以找人领养，女人没了丈夫则注定潦倒一生。"依此解释来说服西方舆论界对中国人的这种求生行为予以谅解，并按照东西方的文化差异求得认同。

应该指出的是，存在着这样一种可能性，那就是这八名中国人根本不具备英语沟通能力，对船长发出的"让妇女和儿童先上船"的命令根本听不懂，他们根本就不知道自己的求生行为是违反当时船上规定的。又因为他们长年工作在船上，了解救生艇的构造，他们就急中生智去救生艇的底下避难，以为这是没有占用救生艇上乘客的座位的合法行为。

今天，我们从史料记录上也能找到三点来说明他们可能真不懂英语。其一，海难时，在 14 号救生艇上获救的中国人 Fang Lang，他苏醒时讲的不是英语。当他发现周围乘客根本听不懂他的语言时，又以伸展手臂的姿势让大家明白他身体恢复知觉了。其二，救生艇上的其他幸存者说，他们好像不懂英文。其三，幸存的乘客后来都要经过美国移民局的逐个审查询问。美国移民局是通过翻译的协助来询问最后幸存的这六名中国人的。

综上所述，他们在面临海难时，也同时面临着语言障碍。

李 瑛
普利尔展览公司

EIGHT CHINESE PASSENGERS ON THE *TITANIC*

Eight Chinese names are recorded in the passenger's list of *Titanic*. They are: Fang Lang, Lee Bing, Ali Lam, Chang Chip, Choong Foo, Len Lam, Ling Hee, and Lee Ling. There have been controversies about how to spell those Chinese passengers' English names for over a hundred years.

At the National Archives of the United States, one can find three signatures —Zhong Jie, Lee Bing, Bing Xin— in Chinese traditional characters among the eight names. Their ages varied from the youngest at 24 years old to the oldest at 37 years old. Bing Lee is the only person who was married, the others were single. The Lams were from Canton and Chinese nationals. The other six were traveling on British passports from Hong Kong. They worked in the boiler rooms of foreign ships.

They were just ordinary passengers on *Titanic*. The reason they boarded *Titanic* was because of the British coal workers' strike, which made them lose their jobs. They later found a new job in a shipping company called the Donald Steamship Company. They went to British Southampton, then boarded *Titanic* en route to New York. According to the original plan, after arriving in New York, they would board the Annetta ship to Cuba, while staying in the ship to work. At that time, Chinese were not allowed to enter the United States based on the Chinese Exclusion Act, although they were processed by U.S. immigration.

The Donald Steamship Company paid in advance for their group tickets. The ticket number was 1601. The fare cost 59 pounds 9 shillings and 11 pence for cabin class - the third class.

The western social class system was also reflected in *Titanic's* cabin levels. The passengers who stayed in the third class would not be allowed to socialize on board with other passengers from first or second class. They could visit the poop deck, but they could not go to the upper deck for sightseeing. These third class passengers were mostly immigrants from all over Europe going to the United States for a new life.

The basic facilities provided in *Titanic* Third Class cabins were likely very enjoyable for passengers. The living conditions were more comfortable. There were big public rooms for men and women and public Smoking Rooms. The cabins were equipped with a spring mattress, pillows, blankets. The room was also equipped with a small washing basin, washstand, wardrobe, and bed heater etc. The food in the Third Class Restaurant was simple, but there was variety: oatmeal, milk, bread, smoked herring, steak, fruit, etc. This was definitely a kind of luxurious life experience for the eight Chinese Passengers. They could not have predicted that just as they started relaxing and entertaining themselves in their rare off-time that a shipwreck would mercilessly end it all.

When the shipwreck occurred, Fang Lang was found lying on a piece of wood. He was the last of the passengers rescued by the No. 14 lifeboat officer Lowe. Fang was already suffering from frozen limbs, but after the lifeboat passengers massaged him, he was restored. When he found the crew around him faint due to fatigue, he took the oars, and kept rowing. Commander Lowe praised him that he "looks like a hero!" With his own practical action, he quickly won the respect of all the passengers on the lifeboat.

Another Chinese, named Choog Foo, climbed into No. 13 lifeboat. Other people— Lee Bing, Ali Lam, Chang Chip, Len Lam, Ling Hee, and Lee Ling — also climbed into different lifeboats. They thought the bottom of the lifeboat was the best place to survive. But Len Lam and Lee Ling, who chose to under the slats of the lifeboat, could not escape from death. The two Chinese may have been crushed to death from the weight of the other passengers. In fact, they also may have died from hypothermia.

On April 15, 1912 at 2:40 am, the ship Carpathia came to rescue the 705 survivors of *Titanic*. They were sent to New York. In the port of New York, only *Titanic* First Class and the Second Class passengers who had handled the formalities were allowed to enter the United States directly. The Third Class passengers would continue to take the Carpathia to Ellis Island, where all the passengers were allowed to disembark. Only the six Chinese were not allowed to enter the United States because of the Chinese Exclusion Act. They were investigated and questioned by the U.S. immigration inspector on board the Carpathia. Then they were sent on the second day directly to the Annetta ship, which was bound to Cuba, to continue to work for the Donald Steamship Company.

On Ellis Island, the six surviving Chinese, except Fang Lang, were questioned , The U.S. media reported the Chinese survivors in an incredible tone. A Chinese Shanghai Declaration newspaper has also relevant reports.

On April 17, 1912, Henry Ford, the director of American-China Special Affairs Association, tried to make a plea for the Chinese people on *Titanic* and justify their behavior. He said to New York Times: "In China, the rescue order is based on men, children and women. This is because the men in China occupy the highest position. If children lost their loved ones, you can find people to adopt them. A woman without a husband is destined to be very poor in her life". According to this explanation, it seemed that this behavior of the Chinese people could be forgiven .

It should be noted that these Chinese people couldn't understand English. Therefore, they didn't really understand the Captain when he issued the command "women and children first". They didn't know that they attempt to save themselves was in violation of the command at the time. They were familiar with ships and lifeboats, and shared a cabin in the bow area. They knew how to survive.

We can only find three indications from the historical records to show that they may not have understood English. Firstly, the Chinese Fang Lang was rescued in lifeboat 14. When he woke up on the life boat, he could only speak Cantonese. When he found the surrounding passengers did not understand his Cantonese, he had to let everyone know he regained consciousness by posing with outstretched arms. He also volunteered to help row the boat and earned the gratitude of Officer Lowe. Secondly, other survivors on lifeboats stated that they did not understand English. Thirdly, when the surviving passengers met the Immigration Department of the United States, the United States immigration service spoke to the six men through an interpreter.

In conclusion, these Chinese passengers had gone through a ship wreck, at the same time, they faced a language barrier while trying to survive the sinking.

.

Ying Li
Premier Exhibitions, Inc.

前言

造船与启航

船上生活

冰山和救援

海底和发现

纪念

图 版
CATALOGUE

Introduction

Construction and Departure

Life On Board Galleries

Iceberg and Rescue

Seabed and Discovery

Memory

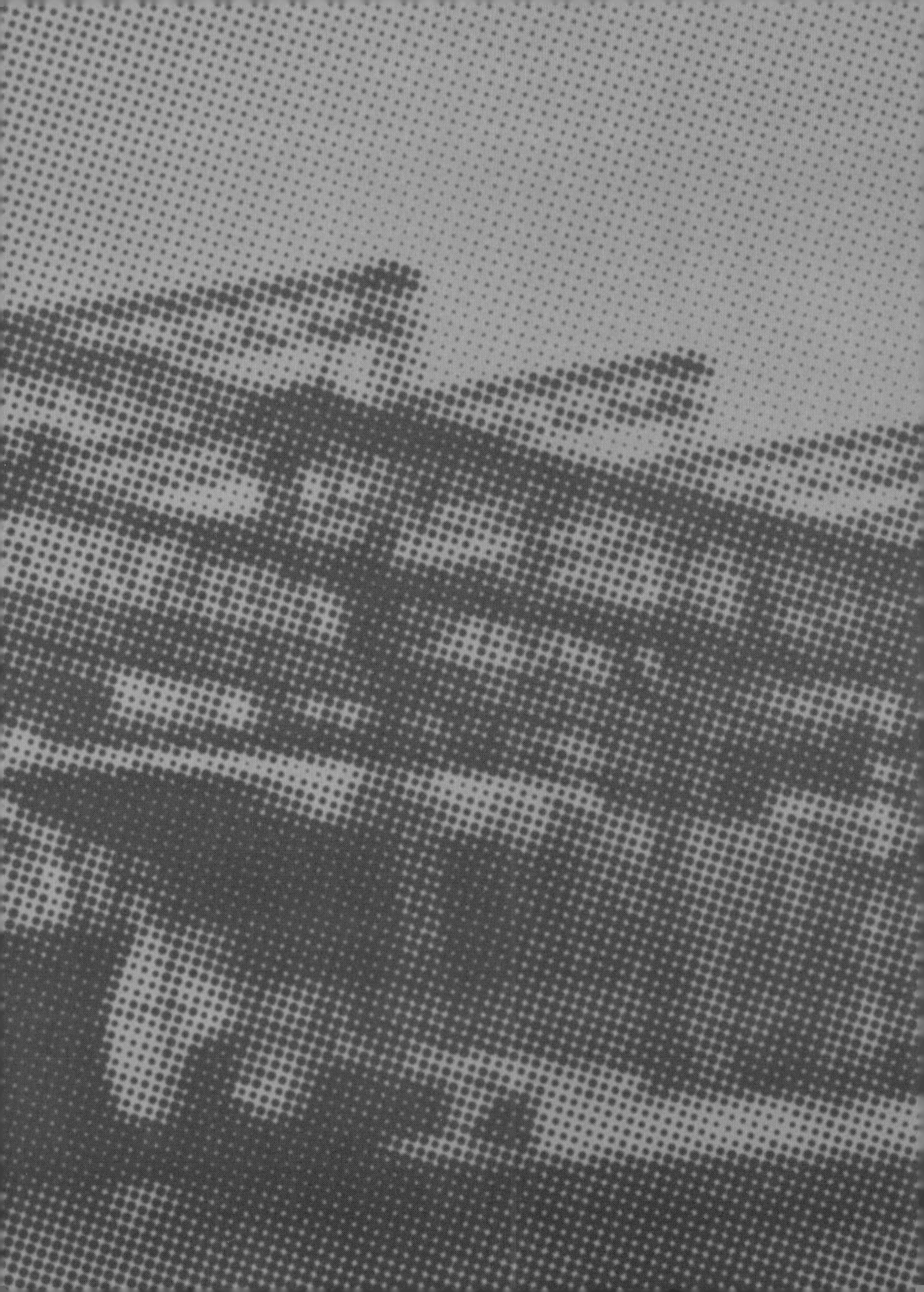

泰坦尼克号邮轮
RMS *Titanic*

客舱甲板
Saloon Deck

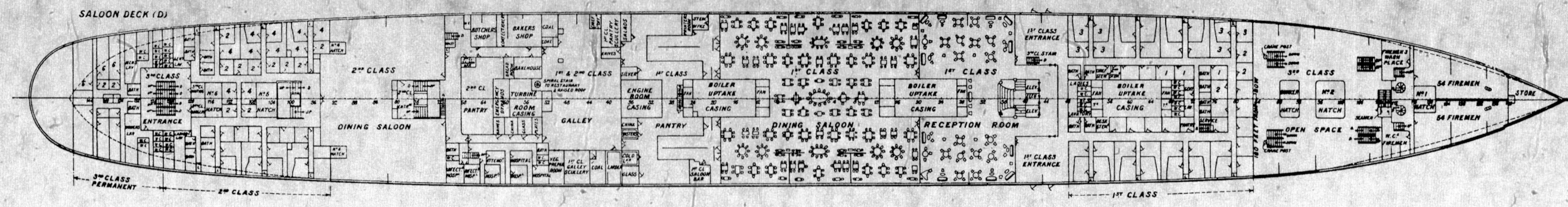

上甲板
Upper Deck

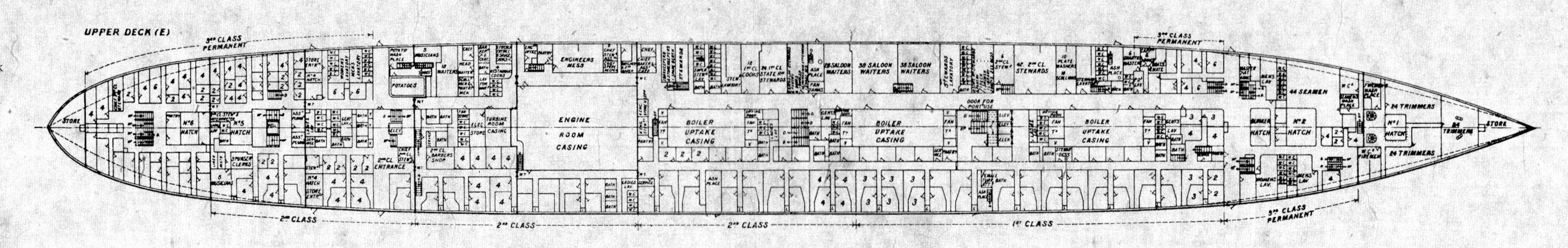

中层甲板
Middle Deck

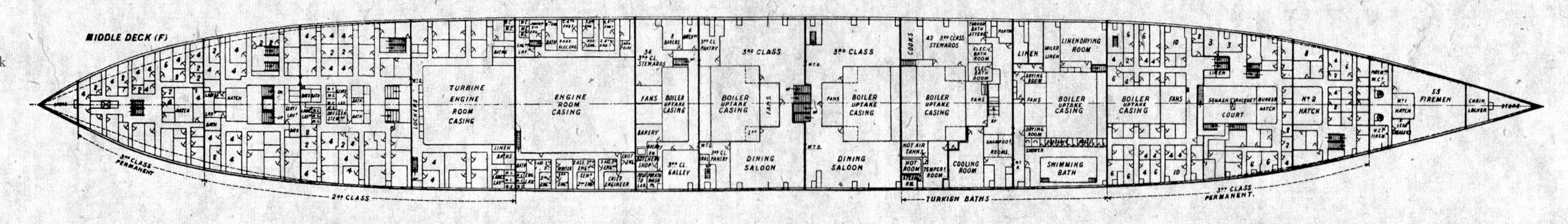

下甲板
Lower Deck

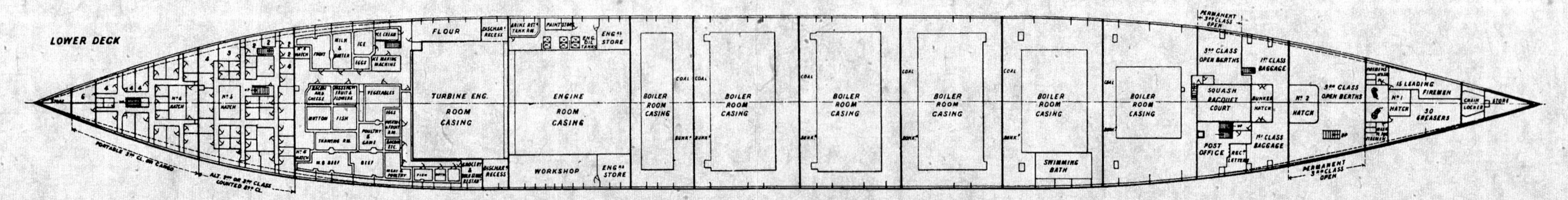

300　　　　　　　400 Feet

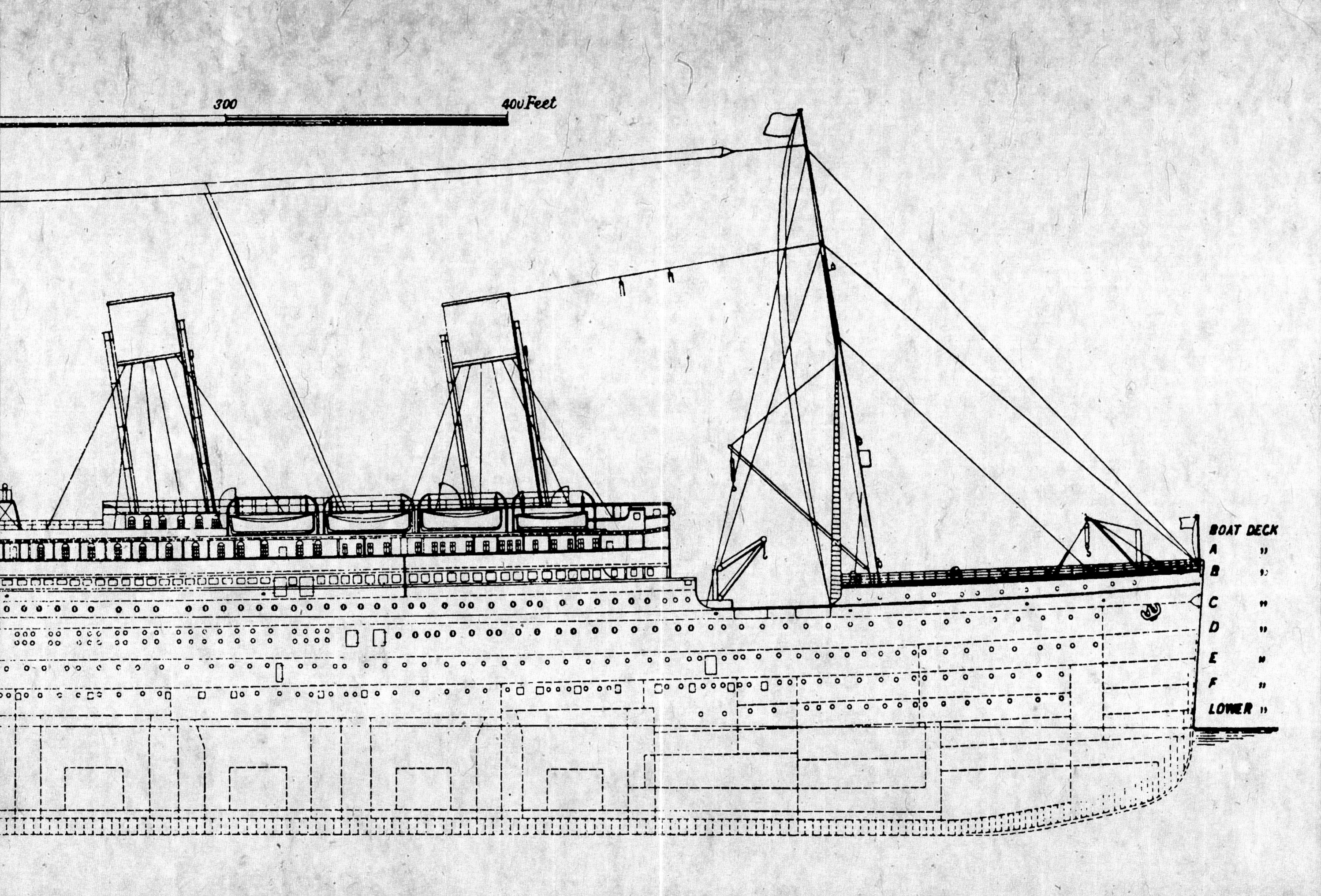

BOAT DECK
A
B
C
D
E
F
LOWER

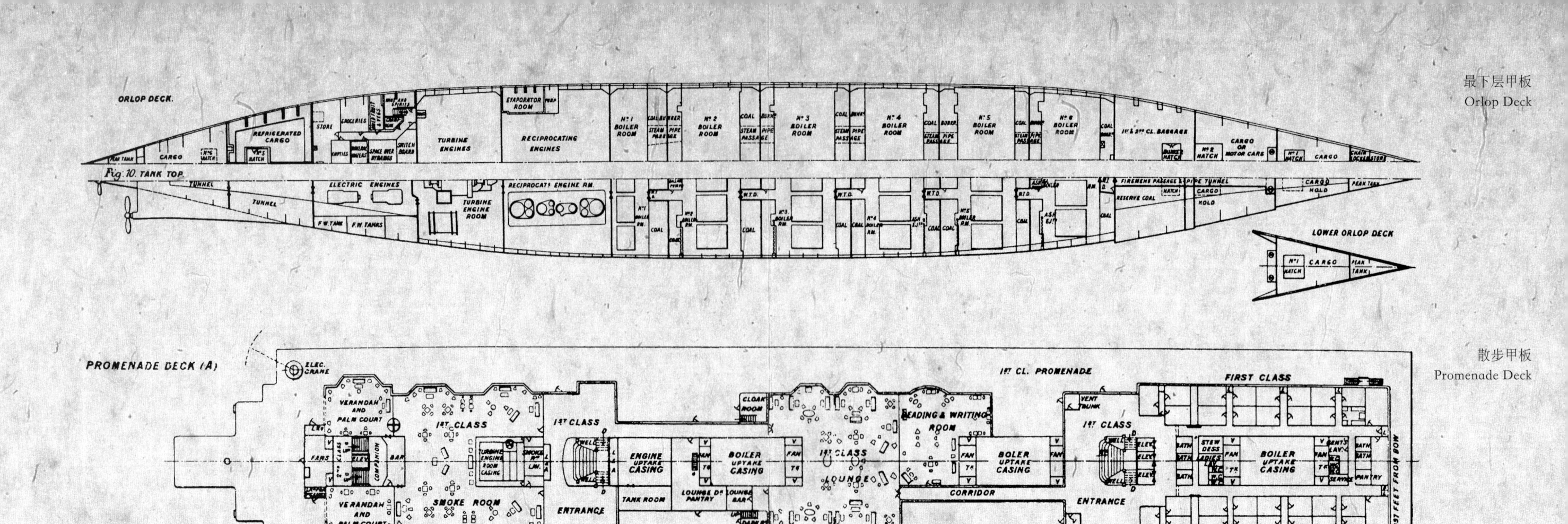

最下层甲板
Orlop Deck

散步甲板
Promenade Deck

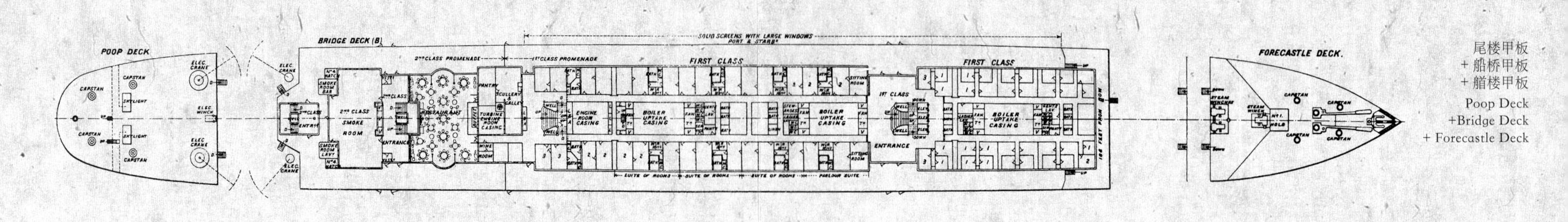

尾楼甲板
+ 船桥甲板
+ 艏楼甲板
Poop Deck
+ Bridge Deck
+ Forecastle Deck

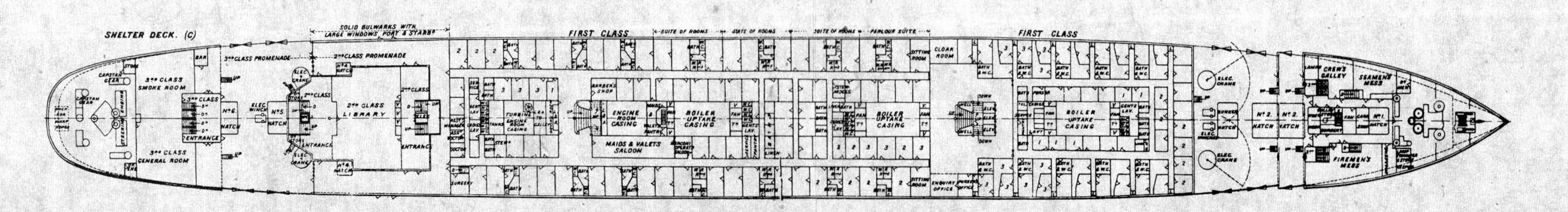

遮蔽甲板
Shelter Deck

前 言

泰坦尼克号豪华邮轮，由英国白星航运公司建造。船体于1907年开始构思设计，1912年首航时在北大西洋沉没。它的诞生，是那个时代最宏伟的文明产物，被认为永不沉没；它的巨大与奢华，被称为"世界工业史上的奇迹"；它的短暂存在，也给世人留下了许多传奇故事和至今未能解开的谜团。

虽然人们一直缅怀着泰坦尼克号感人肺腑的故事，传颂着泰坦尼克号的精神，却从来没有像展览呈现的展品那样，真实而有力，让人产生情感和精神上的共鸣。"泰坦尼克文物精品展"展出了从北大西洋海平面2.5英里（3800米）以下打捞的302件文物。那些看似极其普通的物品，诸如：一只花瓶、一条丝绸领带、一张明信片，都在用无声的语言向我们倾诉着生命的脆弱和亲人的重要；"永不沉没"的骄傲预言被无情的大海吞没的残酷事实又告诫我们：人类不能对科学技术过度依赖；那闪闪发光的金表指针，被北大西洋冰冷的海水掠过，也仿佛叙述着富裕也不能避免悲剧的无奈。

今天，我们纪念泰坦尼克号，并仍然试图去解开它的沉船之谜。我们纪念这些曾经存在的生命，他们因为乘坐泰坦尼克号而被改变了一生的命运！

INTRODUCTION

RMS *Titanic* was built by the British White Star Line Company. It was conceived in 1907 and sank during its maiden voyage in 1912 in the North Atlantic. At the time, it was the largest ship ever built and the largest moving object created by man. It was supposed to be unsinkable. The *Titanic* was huge and luxurious, a miracle in the history of the world. Its brief existence was fraught with the drama of a Greek tragedy. It left behind many stories, legends, and mysteries.

Although people will always remember the touching story of *Titanic*, told and retold, it has never been more poignantly presented than by the artifacts in this exhibition. The *Titanic* exhibition displays 302 cultural relics salvaged from the Atlantic Ocean wreck site, 2.5 miles (3,800 meters) deep. Viewing the exhibition reminds us of our common humanity. Objects as commonplace as a vase, a silk tie and a postcard, are filled with a silent language, reminding us of life's fragility and the importance of loved ones. The proud prediction that the Ship would never sink was destroyed by the merciless sea. The story of the *Titanic* reminds us that men cannot rely too much on science and technology. A once shimmering gold watch, its hands swept away by the frigid waters of the North Atlantic, warns us that wealth does not insulate against tragedy.

Today, we commemorate *Titanic* and those who boarded the Ship for its fateful maiden voyage as we continue to try and unravel the mystery of the wreck.

造船与启航

泰坦尼克号建造于北爱尔兰的最大城市贝尔法斯特的哈兰德·沃尔夫造船厂。船体于1911年5月31日下水。它也是白星航运(White Star Line)公司在同一造船厂建造的第二艘奥林匹克级别的轮船。在当时是最大、最著名的载人轮船。泰坦尼克号长269米，宽28米，重约46328000千克。船上有899名船员，可以运载3,300名乘客。因为它也运送邮件，所以也叫皇家邮轮泰坦尼克号。

1912年4月10日上午，泰坦尼克号鸣笛起锚，由船长Edward J. Smith掌舵，以庄严宏大的气势开始了它的处女航。在法国瑟堡与爱尔兰昆士城停船搭载临时乘客及接收托运邮件后，泰坦尼克号劈波斩浪，穿过北大西洋，开往纽约。

CONSTRUCTION AND DEPARTURE

The *Titanic* was built at Harland & Wolff's Queens Island shipyard. Launched on May 31, 1911, it was the second Olympic-class ship built in the shipyard by White Star Line. The largest and the most well-known of the three ships, it measured 269 meters long, 28 meters wide and 46,328 Gross Registered Tons. . There were 899 crew on board . It was available for 3,300 passengers. It was also known as Royal Mail Steamer *Titanic*, for it also shipped mail.

Morning of April 10,1912, *Titanic* sounded her whistles, slipped her mooring lines and, majestic and powerful, began her maiden voyage with Captain Edward J. Smith at the helm. After stops to collect additional passengers and mail in Cherbourg, France and Queenstown, Ireland, the Ship struck out across the North Atlantic for New York.

桅杆挂钟
来源： 英国
年代： 爱德华时期，1901-1914
尺寸： 34.29 厘米 x 37.46 厘米

Crow's Nest Bell
Origin: United Kingdom
Period: Edwardian Period, 1901-1914
Size: 34.29 cm x 37.46 cm

这尊铜钟最初悬挂在泰坦尼克前桅的桅杆（瞭望台）上，用于发出警告和报警，同时用于日常计时。4月14日，瞭望员敲了三下警钟，警告正前方发现冰山。由此泰坦尼克号的沉没厄运开始了。

This bronze bell originally hung over Titanic's crow's nest (the lookout's cage) on the foremast. It was used for warnings and alarms, as well as general time keeping. On April 14, Lookout Fleet rang this bell three times, warning the bridge of an iceberg straight ahead. Thus began the fateful sinking of RMS Titanic.

舷窗框

来源： 英国
年代： 爱德华时期，1901-1914
尺寸： 55.88 厘米 x 71.12 厘米 x 0.32 厘米

Porthole Frame

Origin: United Kingdom
Period: Edwardian Period, 1901-1914
Size: 55.88 cm x 71.12 cm x 0.32 cm

这是泰坦尼克号的标准舷窗框。框边的螺丝扣很重，叫做"舷窗扣"，用于密封舷窗。舷窗玻璃已遗失。泰坦尼克号要求乘客使用时，由乘务员协助打开。因为一旦玻璃脱落会划破手指，所以船上的一名外科医生给它起了个"舷窗指"的绰号。

This is a standard porthole frame from the Ship. The heavy turnbuckles at the edge of the frame, called "porthole dogs," ensured that the porthole was watertight. The glass has been lost. *Titanic's* stewards insisted passengers ask for assistance, because if dropped, the result could be a broken finger, a condition steamship surgeons nicknamed "porthole thumb."

引擎过滤框

来源： 英国
年代： 爱德华时期，1901-1914
尺寸： 16.51 厘米 x 68.58 厘米

Engine Filter Frame

Origin: United Kingdom
Period: Edwardian Period, 1901-1914
Size: 16.51 cm x 68.58 cm

铜制框，形状如硬币，内有金属鼓，厚绒布过滤掉介质中的杂质成分。这个过滤框是用来将从冷凝器中流出的水过滤到锅炉中，通过互换引擎去除掉像油一样的杂质。

This bronze frame, one of many that were stacked like coins inside a metal drum, held a terry cloth filtering medium through which water was forced. The frame was used to filter feed water from the condensers back to the boilers, removing impurities like oil that the steam picked up as it passed through the reciprocating engines.

工具手柄

来源： 欧洲
年代： 爱德华时期，1901-1914
尺寸： ① 9.52 厘米 x 2.54 厘米
② 25.71 厘米 x 2.69 厘米 x 2.22 厘米
③ 25.71 厘米 x 2.22 厘米 x 1.27 厘米

Tool Handles

Origin: Europe
Period: Edwardian Period, 1901-1914
Size: ① 9.52 cm x 2.54 cm
② 25.71 cm x 2.69 cm x 2.22 cm
③ 25.71 cm x 2.22 cm x 1.27 cm

①

②

③

船上二等舱和三等舱的很多乘客是技术工人，如鞋匠、锡匠和木匠。他们携带的工具对于他们在美国建造新家园至关重要。这些工具是在皮手袋里发现的，金属部分在海水中被腐蚀掉了。

Many of the Ship's second and third class passengers were skilled laborers, such as shoemakers, tinsmiths, and carpenters. The tools they carried were vital to establishing themselves in their new home in America. These tool handles were found inside a leather bag, the metal parts corroded in the salt water.

船上铆钉、螺栓、螺母

来源： 欧洲
年代： 爱德华时期，1901-1914
尺寸： ① 5.87 厘米 x 4.7625 厘米
② 4.76 厘米 x 3.49 厘米
③ 5.08 厘米 x 3.17 厘米 x 1.59 厘米
④ 8.09 厘米 x 2.69 厘米 x 3.01 厘米
⑤ 4.12 厘米 x 3.01 厘米 x 1.58 厘米

Ship Rivets, Bolt and Nut

Origin: United Kingdom
Period: Edwardian Period, 1901-1914
Size: ① 5.87 cm x 4.7625 cm
② 4.76 cm x 3.49 cm
③ 5.08 cm x 3.17 cm x 1.59 cm
④ 8.09 cm x 2.69 cm x 3.01 cm
⑤ 4.12 cm x 3.01 cm x 1.58 cm

泰坦尼克号船体是由成千上万片一英寸厚的钢板组成的，钢板由三百多万只铆钉固定。由于铆钉数量巨大，需要昂贵的手工铆钉安装团队来完成。泰坦尼克号的建造全部选用新型的、更快捷、更稳定的水压铆接技术。因为不是船上所有部件都可以使用庞大的机器完成，在机器难以抵达的区域，特别是弯曲和末端部分仍需要使用旧式手工锤凿方法铆入。

铆钉是双头的，可以从两端同时锤凿，以确保钢板间组合在一起。由于船体裂开，很多铆钉因巨大的压力从一端脱落。

Titanic's hull consists of thousands of one-inch-thick steel plates secured to its framework by more than three million rivets. Due to the vast number of rivets and the high cost of skilled hand-riveting teams, *Titanic's* builders adopted the new, faster, and more consistent technique of hydraulic riveting. The bulky machinery could not be used on all sections of the Ship, however, hard-to-reach areas, particularly in the bow and stern, still needed to be riveted by the old hand-hammering method.

Rivets were double-ended from being hit on both ends to secure the steel panels together. As the Ship ripped apart, many of the rivets sheared off on one end due to the extreme pressure.

39

4月6日星期六，从南安普敦启航的四天前，泰坦尼克号开始招募船员和装运货物。不久，成箱的虾、核桃、书、水果、天鹅绒、法国白兰地和各类必需品被陆续装上客船。

泰坦尼克号的船员在港口使用这个货钩吊起货物和必需品运到船甲板上。这件铁砝码用于在大风中固定空钩。

On Saturday April 6, four days before setting sail from Southampton, crew recruitment was underway and general cargo began to arrive at the dockside for loading. Soon the cargo holds would be full of crates of ostrich plumes, shelled walnuts, books, fruit preserves, velvet, cognac, and all manner of products one would expect to find in the hold of an express passenger liner in 1912.

While in port, *Titanic's* crew used this hook to hoist cargo and provisions onto the Ship's decks. The extra metal weight helped keep the empty hook steady in strong wind.

生铁货钩
来源： 英国
年代： 爱德华时期，1901-1914
尺寸： 136.52 厘米 x 24.13 厘米 x 22.22 厘米

Cast Iron Cargo Hook
Origin: United Kingdom
Period: Edwardian Period, 1901-1914
  Size: 136.52 cm x 24.13 cm x 22.22 cm

格莱斯顿皮袋和钥匙

来源： 英国
年代： 爱德华时期，1901-1914
尺寸： ① 52.07 厘米 x 25.4 厘米 x 24.13 厘米
② 8.57 厘米 x 3.81 厘米

Leather Gladstone Bag and Key

Origin: United Kingdom
Period: Edwardian Period, 1901-1914
Size: ① 52.07 cm x 25.4 cm x 24.13 cm
② 8.57 cm x 3.81 cm

①

②

轮船撞击冰山后，很多头等舱乘客立即冲向乘务长办公室拿回他们的贵重物品。乘务长及其助理尽量将物品归还给乘客。当接到弃船命令后，他们全力疏散乘客乘坐船上的救生船，同时将剩余的物品装进格莱斯顿式旅行提包。锁好保险箱后，将提包带上救生船，继续分发剩下的贵重物品，然而很多珠宝首饰随泰坦尼克号一同沉入了海底。1987 年，RMS *Titanic*, Inc. 公司探险队打捞出来的格莱斯顿旅行提包里装有珠宝首饰、银行券、金币和金表。提包皮革制作过程添加的化学物质，使得包中易损的纸币和标牌保存完好。

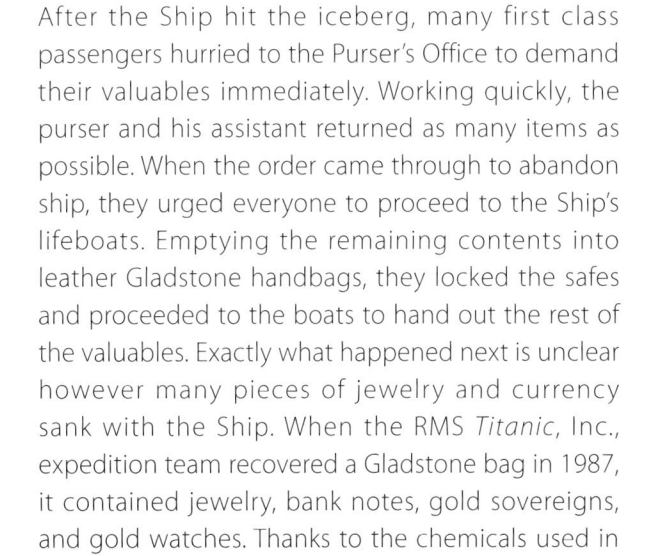

After the Ship hit the iceberg, many first class passengers hurried to the Purser's Office to demand their valuables immediately. Working quickly, the purser and his assistant returned as many items as possible. When the order came through to abandon ship, they urged everyone to proceed to the Ship's lifeboats. Emptying the remaining contents into leather Gladstone handbags, they locked the safes and proceeded to the boats to hand out the rest of the valuables. Exactly what happened next is unclear however many pieces of jewelry and currency sank with the Ship. When the RMS *Titanic*, Inc., expedition team recovered a Gladstone bag in 1987, it contained jewelry, bank notes, gold sovereigns, and gold watches. Thanks to the chemicals used in the tanning process of the bag, even fragile paper currency notes and tags were preserved.

博拉博拉岛明信片

来源： 博拉博拉岛
年代： 爱德华时期，1901-1914
尺寸： 13.97 厘米 x 8.89 厘米

Souvenir Postcard of Bora Bora

Origin: Bora Bora
Period: Edwardian Period, 1901-1914
Size: 13.97 cm x 8.89 cm

在欧文先生的随身物品中发现了 100 多张明信片。这张描绘岛上居民跳舞的明信片说明他曾到过波利尼西亚 (Polynesia) 旅游。明信片是手绘上色的，至今仍保存完好。

Over one hundred postcards were found with Mr. Howard Irwin's belongings. This souvenir postcard of dancing islanders shows he made a trip to Polynesia. The postcard is hand colored and in extremely good condition.

白星航运行李保险袋

来源: 英国
年代: 爱德华时期，1901-1914
尺寸: 37.46 厘米 x 26.03 厘米

White Star Line Baggage Insurance Packet

Origin: United Kingdom
Period: Edwardian Period, 1901-1914
Size: 37.46 cm x 26.03 cm

这个已拆封的信封是从弗兰兹·帕尔鲍姆 (Franz Pulbaum) 的随身行李中找到的，原本装有白星航运保险行李标签。白星航运鼓励乘客根据信封上的指南，按规定标准购买行李保险。

This unfolded envelope originally contained White Star Line insurance baggage labels and was recovered from a suitcase belonging to passenger Franz Pulbaum. The White Star Line encouraged passengers to purchase baggage insurance at standard rates as described in the instructions on this envelope.

船上生活

爱德华时代的文化体现了巨大的等级差异。在泰坦尼克号船上，头等舱、二等舱和三等舱的乘客在舒适度上存在明显的贫富差异。来自泰坦尼克号沉船遗址的文物，包括不同厨房的壶、碟以及乘客的个人物品，讲述着泰坦尼克号上著名乘客的故事。

LIFE ON BOARD

Edwardian culture embodied a great class differentiation. On *Titanic*, cabins for first, second and third-class passengers detail the differences in comfort for the very rich and the poor. Objects removed from the wreckage of *Titanic* include pots and dishes from the different galleys, as well as many personal belongings of passengers. Stories of some of *Titanic*'s most notable passengers are highlighted in this section.

六枚爱德华七世和乔治五世纪念金币

来源： 英国
年代： 爱德华时期，1907-1911
尺寸： 直径 2.22 厘米

Six Gold Sovereigns of King Edward VII and King George V

Origin:　United Kingdom
Period:　Edwardian Period, 1907 -1911
　Size:　diam. 2.22 cm

硬币

此处展出的硬币来自英国、美国和比利时。大多数硬币是在乘务长办公室格莱斯顿式旅行提包里发现的，还发现了其他硬币，其中包括俄罗斯卢布、法国法郎和土耳其里拉。

Coins

The coins displayed here are from the United Kingdom, United States, and Belgium. The majority of coins were found in a leather Gladstone bag of purser's office. Other examples of coins were found include a Russian ruble, French franc, and a Turkish para.

这六枚金币是 1907 年至 1911 年为纪念乔治五世和爱德华七世国王而铸造的英国纪念币的代表。金币背面印有乔治骑马杀龙的图案。一枚纪念币价值为一英镑。

These are six examples of many gold British sovereigns that were minted between 1907 and 1911 in honor of King George V and King Edward VII. The reverse of the coins shows St. George on a horse slaying a dragon. The value of a commemorative coin is one pound.

45

50 美分硬币

　来源：　美国
　年代：　爱德华时期，1901 年
　尺寸：　直径 3.02 厘米

U. S. Half Dollar

Origin: 　United States
Period: 　Edwardian Period, 1901
　Size: 　diam. 3.02 cm

这枚 1900 年的硬币被称为"摩根"美元。铸造时美国货币与美国金银储备挂钩。每枚摩根币重 1.04 盎司，由 90% 银和 10% 铜铸成。

This dollar coin from 1900 is called a "Morgan" dollar, and was minted when US currency was still tied to the country's supply of gold and silver. Morgan dollars each weighed 1.04 oz and were composed of 90% silver and 10% copper.

1 美元硬币

来源： 美国
年代： 爱德华时期，1900 年
尺寸： 直径 3.81 厘米

U. S. Dollar

Origin: United States
Period: Edwardian Period, 1900
Size: diam. 3.81 cm

10 美分硬币

来源： 美国
年代： 爱德华时期，1900 年
尺寸： 直径 1.74 厘米

U. S. Dime

Origin: United States
Period: Edwardian Period, 1900
Size: diam. 1.74 cm

25 美分硬币

来源： 美国
年代： 爱德华时期，1911 年
尺寸： 直径 2.38 厘米

U. S. Quarter

Origin: United States
Period: Edwardian Period, 1911
Size: diam. 2.38 cm

半克朗英国硬币，维多利亚

来源： 英国
年代： 爱德华时期，1900 年
尺寸： 直径 3.17 厘米

U. K. Half Crown, Victoria

Origin: United Kingdom
Period: Edwardian Period, 1900
Size: diam. 3.17 cm

1 便士英国硬币，爱德华七世

来源： 英国
年代： 爱德华时期，1910 年
尺寸： 直径 3.17 厘米

U. K. One Penny, Edwardus VII

Origin: United Kingdom
Period: Edwardian Period, 1910
Size: diam. 3.17 cm

1 先令英国硬币，爱德华七世

来源： 英国
年代： 爱德华时期，1910 年
尺寸： 直径 2.38 厘米

U. K. Shilling, Edwardus VII

Origin: United Kingdom
Period: Edwardian Period, 1910
Size: diam. 2.38 cm

6 便士英国硬币，爱德华七世

来源：　英国
年代：　爱德华时期，1909 年
尺寸：　直径 1.9 厘米

U. K. Six Pence, Edwardus VII

Origin:　United Kingdom
Period:　Edwardian Period, 1909
　Size:　diam. 1.9 cm

2 先令英国硬币，爱德华七世

来源： 英国
年代： 爱德华时期，1908 年
尺寸： 直径 2.86 厘米

U. K. Florin/Two Shillings, Edwardus VII

Origin: United Kingdom
Period: Edwardian Period, 1908
Size: diam. 2.86 cm

10 分比利时硬币

来源： 比利时
年代： 爱德华时期，1908 年
尺寸： 直径 2.22 厘米

10 Centimes, Belgium coin

Origin: Belgium
Period: Edwardian Period, 1908
Size: diam. 2.22 cm

半克朗英国硬币，爱德华七世

来源：　英国
年代：　爱德华时期，1907 年
尺寸：　直径 3.17 厘米

U. K. Half Crown, Edwardus VII

Origin: 　United Kingdom
Period: 　Edwardian Period, 1907
Size: 　diam. 3.17 cm

纸 币

一百多年前，私人银行和美国联邦政府都发行纸币。各地银行印刷这些"期票"，以国债的形式按比例认购国债。许多欧洲银行不愿接受大量无名的美国银行印制发行的货币，以致美国游客要经常携带英镑。1912 年过后不久，美国修改了货币法，联邦政府独享印钞权。

Paper Currency

One hundred years ago, both private banks and the U.S. Federal Government issued paper money. Banks in various cities printed these "promissory notes" in proportion to the national debt they underwrote. The large number of obscure U.S. banks issuing money made many European banks reluctant to accept American paper currency. As a result, American travelers often carried British pounds. Shortly after 1912, U.S. currency laws changed and the right to print money went to the federal government alone.

美国法定货币纸币

在现代的法定货币制度形成之前，像这样的法定纸币与黄金的价值挂钩。1971年，他们被现在使用的美元钞票所取代。这个法定货币债券印制于1907年。

American Legal Tender Notes

Before the modern fiat system of currency, Legal Tender Notes like this one were tied to the value of gold. In 1971, they were replaced by the modern U.S. dollar bill. This Legal Tender Note was printed in 1907.

5 美元面值法定纸币，樵夫

来源： 美国
年代： 爱德华时期，1907 年
尺寸： 18.89 厘米 x 7.78 厘米

U.S. $5 Legal Tender Note, Woodchoppers

Origin: United States
Period: Edwardian Period, 1907
Size: 18.89 cm x 7.78 cm

5 美元面值法定纸币，樵夫

来源： 美国
年代： 爱德华时期，1907 年
尺寸： 18.89 厘米 x 7.78 厘米

U.S. $5 Legal Tender Note, Woodchoppers

Origin: United States
Period: Edwardian Period, 1907
Size: 18.89 cm x 7.78 cm

美国国家银行券

国家银行券是由美国政府指定的国家银行发行的现钞纸币。1935年停用。

U.S. National Bank Note

National bank notes were United States currency issued by banks chartered by the United States Government. They were retired as a currency type in 1935.

5美元面值银行券，本杰明·哈里森 (Benjamin Harrison)

来源： 美国
年代： 爱德华时期，1902年
尺寸： 18.73 厘米 x 7.94 厘米

U.S. $5 Bank Note, Benjamin Harrison

Origin: United States
Period: Edwardian Period, 1902
Size: 18.73 cm x 7.94 cm

10 美元面值银行券，西法戈
(West Fargo)

来源： 美国
年代： 爱德华时期，1902 年
尺寸： 17.94 厘米 x 7.78 厘米

U.S. $10 Bank Note, West Fargo

Origin: United States
Period: Edwardian Period, 1902
Size: 17.94 cm x 7.78 cm

10 美元面值银行券，威廉·麦金利总统
(William McKinley)

来源： 美国
年代： 爱德华时期，1902 年
尺寸： 18.41 厘米 x 7.94 厘米

U.S. $10 Bank Note, President William McKinley

Origin: United States
Period: Edwardian Period, 1902
Size: 18.41 cm x 7.94 cm

55

美国银券

在 1878 年—1923 年间，大尺寸银券由美国财政部印制。1908 年 10 美元系列的银券上印有副总统 Thomas A. Hendricks 的肖像，这是美国唯一印有副总统肖像的货币。肖像外圈的形状使这个货币有个绰号叫"墓碑券"。

American Silver Certificate

Large-size Silver Certificates were printed by the U.S. Treasury from 1878 to 1928. The 1908 series of $10 silver certificates featured Vice President Thomas A. Hendricks, and is the only U.S. currency to feature a Vice President. The shape of the portrait enclosure has given this currency the nickname of "Tombstone Note."

10 美元面值银券，副总统托马斯·A. 亨德里克
(Thomas A. Hendricks)

来源： 美国
年代： 爱德华时期，1908 年
尺寸： 18.73 厘米 x 7.78 厘米

U.S. $10 Silver Certificate, Vice President Thomas A. Hendricks

Origin: United States
Period: Edwardian Period, 1908
Size: 18.73 cm x 7.78 cm

10 美元面值金券，第一任美财长
麦克·希尔格斯 (Michael Hillegas)

来源： 美国
年代： 爱德华时期，1907 年
尺寸： 18.57 厘米 x 7.78 厘米

U.S. $10 Gold Certificate, First U.S. Treasurer Michael Hillegas

Origin: United States
Period: Edwardian Period, 1907
Size: 18.57 cm x 7.78 cm

首饰配件
Jewelry and Accessories

金怀表，背面有扭索状装饰图案

来源： 英国
年代： 爱德华时期，1912 年
尺寸： 13.6 厘米 x 18.9 厘米 x 3.8 厘米

Gold Pocket Watch, guilloche decoration on back

Origin: United Kingdom
Period: Edwardian Period, 1912
Size: 13.6 cm x 18.9 cm x 3.8 cm

这块怀表属于南非开普殖民地一位 60 岁的旅馆老板托马斯·威廉·所罗门·布朗 (Thomas William Solomon Brown)，当时他和妻子、女儿住在二等舱。怀表的背面有一个美丽的连结环图案，是少数几只仍有指针显示时间的表之一，怀表在船下沉时停摆。布朗先生在事故中遇难。

This pocket watch belonged to Thomas William Solomon Brown, a 60-year-old hotelier from the Cape Colony, South Africa. Brown was traveling in second class with his wife and daughter. The watch has a beautiful guilloche pattern on the back, and is one of the few watches that still has the hands showing the time the watch stopped working during the sinking. Mr. Brown did not survive the sinking.

怀表后壳或小装饰品
来源： 法国
年代： 爱德华时期，1910 年
尺寸： 4.45 厘米 x 1.91 厘米

Open Locket or Charm
Origin:　France
Period:　Edwardian Period, 1910
Size:　4.45 cm x 1.91 cm

怀表后壳或小装饰品是从打捞上来的一个小绸物袋中与其他一些小文物一起发现的。它是由黄金制作的，周边环绕着小石榴石。表壳中心用法文刻着日期"4 Août 1910"，即 1910 年 8 月 4 日。

This open locket or charm was recovered from a small taffeta bag with other a few artifacts. It is made of gold with a surround of small garnets. The center is engraved in French with a date "4 Août 1910" which translates as 4 August 1910.

女式白金蓝宝石钻戒

来源： 美国
年代： 爱德华时期，1912 年
尺寸： 顶部 1.18 厘米 x 1.07 厘米；直径 1.9 厘米

Lady's Gold and Platinum Ring with Sapphire and Diamonds

Origin: United States
Period: Edwardian Period, 1912
Size: top 1.18 cm x 1.07 cm; diam. 1.9 cm

这枚特别的戒指是1987年从泰坦尼克号沉船遗址中打捞上来的。手工制作，工艺精细。蓝宝石及钻石戒指用18K黄金和铂金制作，嵌有一颗天然蓝宝石和多颗小钻石，呈圆润的花瓣形。

英国素来以蓝宝石象征爱情。阿尔伯特（Albert）亲王在结婚前一天送给维多利亚女王的就是蓝宝石钻戒。查尔斯（Charles）王储也曾将美丽的蓝宝石钻戒作为订婚戒指送给戴安娜王妃。同样，蓝宝石钻戒也被用作威廉王子和凯瑟琳·米德尔顿的订婚戒指。

This exceptional ring was recovered from *Titanic's* wreck site in 1987. It is hand-constructed with fine detail and craftsmanship. The sapphire and diamond ring is comprised of 18-karat yellow gold and platinum with a natural blue sapphire and multiple small diamonds in the pear-shaped petals.

The British have a long-running love affair with sapphires. Prince Albert presented Queen Victoria with a sapphire and diamond ring the day before their wedding. Prince Charles presented to Lady Diana a beautiful sapphire and diamond engagement ring which was also used in for the engagement of Prince William and Catherine Middleton.

心形吊坠项链

来源： 英国
年代： 爱德华时期，1912 年
尺寸： 23.49 厘米 x 2.86 厘米

Open Heart Necklace

Origin: United Kingdom
Period: Edwardian Period, 1912
Size: 23.49 cm x 2.86 cm

这个迷人的项链有一个用玻璃和珍珠作为装饰的银制心形吊坠，链子是 9K 的黄金链。

This intriguing necklace features a silver open heart pendant with glass and pearl decoration. It is attached to a 9-karat gold chain.

纯金钻石飘带胸针

来源：美国
年代：爱德华时期，1912 年
尺寸：2.5 厘米 x 1.54 厘米

Lady's Gold and Diamond Ribbon Brooch

Origin: United States
Period: Edwardian Period, 1912
Size: 2.5 cm x 1.54 cm

飘带或蝴蝶结形胸针自 17 世纪以来在欧洲曾经非常流行。这是一个14K黄金的蝴蝶结状的胸针，中心镶有一颗用旧式切割法切割的钻石，另一端镶有另一颗用同样方式切割的钻石。这种类型的胸针在维多利亚时代再次流行起来，成为英国皇室成员之间互赠礼物的选择。

The ribbon or bow-knot brooch has been popular in Europe since the 1700s. This is a single 14-karat bow-knot set with one old mine-cut diamond in the center and one old mine-cut drop diamond drop. This type of brooch was popularized again during the Victorian period when it became a gift of choice between members of the British Royal family.

镶有玛瑙和钻石的金纽扣盖（一对）
来源： 英国
年代： 爱德华时期，1910 年
尺寸： 高 1.27 厘米；直径 1.9 厘米

Set of Two Gold, Onyx, and Diamond Button Cover
Origin: United Kingdom
Period: Edwardian Period, 1910
Size: h. 1.27 cm; diam. 1.9 cm

这对用于装饰的纽扣盖采用 18K 金边框镶嵌钻石，背衬黑玛瑙。鉴于装饰质量，它们极有可能是属于头等舱的某位男士。

This pair of button covers or studs are made of 18-karat gold and have bezel set diamonds with black onyx backings. Given the decorative quality of these objects, they most likely belonged to a first-class gentleman.

许多泰坦尼克号头等舱乘客喜欢携带他们最漂亮的珠宝首饰在晚上佩戴。在航程中,有些人与泰坦尼克号总乘务长赫伯特·麦克尔罗伊(Herbert McElroy)一起对他们的贵重物品进行安全检查,也有的乘客把携带的贵重物品放在钱袋里或者藏起来。打捞上来的黄金和珐琅连结环袖扣和领扣共有三套,这是其中一套。每一套都有不同的珐琅彩。

Many of *Titanic's* first class passengers brought their finest jewels to wear in the evening while at sea. Some checked their valuables with *Titanic's* Chief Purser, Herbert McElroy, for safekeeping during the voyage. Other passengers carried their valuables in money belts or hid them. This set of gold and enamel guilloche cufflinks and collar buttons was one of three sets recovered together. Each set has a different enamel color.

袖扣、领扣(一套)
来源: 欧洲
年代: 爱德华时期,1912 年
尺寸: 袖扣 1.59 厘米 x 0.74 厘米;领扣直径 0.95 厘米

Set of Cufflinks and Collar Buttons
Origin: Europe
Period: Edwardian Period, 1912
Size: cufflinks 1.59 cm x 0.74 cm; buttons diam. 0.95 cm

狐狸头金别针

来源： 英国
年代： 爱德华时期，1912 年
尺寸： 高 16.35 厘米；直径 5.08 厘米

Stick Pin with Fox Head

Origin:　United Kingdom
Period:　Edwardian Period, 1912
　Size:　h. 16.35 cm ; diam. 5.08 cm

这款精细的 14K 黄金狐狸头别针有两个小的凸面宝石的眼睛，看起来像是玻璃做的。头部和针部焊接在一起，头部由手工精雕细琢，精细的雕工和眼神特色鲜明。狐狸在英国非常流行，象征狩猎。

This fine 14-karat yellow gold fox scarf or stick pin has two small round cabochon eyes which appear to be glass. The pin was cast and assembled, and the head was hand etched for detail. The etching and eyes give this pin definite character. The fox was a popular hunting symbol in England.

银扣木珠项链

来源： 英国
年代： 爱德华时期，1912 年
尺寸： 长 147 厘米

Bead Necklace with Silver Stamp

Origin: United Kingdom
Period: Edwardian Period, 1912
Size: l. 147 cm

这串双层木珠项链很可能是一位头等舱乘客佩戴的。项链的珠子是木制的，末端连接扣是一个银制的信封，上面刻有"邮戳"字样，伯明翰制造。

This double strand beaded necklace is a piece of custume jewelry most likely worn by a first class passenger. The necklace features wooden beads and a silver envelope with a hinged lid on which the word "STAMP" has been engraved. The envelope was used to hold stamps and was made in Birmingham, UK.

①

②

大象吊坠和领夹

来源： 英国
年代： 爱德华时期，1912 年
尺寸： ① 2.22 厘米 x 0.63 厘米 x 2.54 厘米
② 2.22 厘米 x 1.90 厘米 x 0.47 厘米

Elephant Pendant and Collar Clip

Orig in: United Kingdom
Period: Edwardian Period, 1912
Size: ① 2.22 cm x 0.63 cm x 2.54 cm
② 2.22 cm x 1.90 cm x 0.47 cm

这件大象吊坠是从一个制作精良的皮箱里的盒子中找到的。它可能是怀表饰物，由木头制成，中心孔被玻璃覆盖。14K 的黄金别针可用来夹领带，中间的珍珠或宝石装饰已缺失。

Recovered from a box in a well-made leather suitcase, this elephant pendant—or perhaps watch fob, is made of wood with a central hole covered by glass. The collar clip is a simple ornament and would have held a pearl or emi-precious stones.

68

美容和个人护理

Grooming and Personal Care

头等舱夜壶

来源： 英国
年代： 爱德华时期，1912 年
尺寸： 高 11.75 厘米；直径 19.68 厘米

First Class Chamber Pot

Origin: United Kingdom
Period: Edwardian Period, 1912
Size: h. 11.75 cm; diam. 19.68 cm

白星航运在船舱里给乘客提供了夜壶，以防晕船、呕吐等突发情况。

White Star Line provided chamber pots in cabins in case passengers experienced a sudden bout of seasickness.

香水瓶

来源： 英国
年代： 爱德华时期，1912 年
尺寸： 11.43 厘米 x 3.81 厘米

Perfume Bottle

Origin: United Kingdom
Period: Edwardian Period, 1912
Size: 11.43 cm x 3.81 cm

这个透明的玻璃香水瓶有一个皇冠形的瓶塞。

This clear glass perfume bottle has a crown-shaped stopper.

二等舱里的陶瓷肥皂盒安装在船舱洗手盆上方的柜子上。

In second class, ceramic soap boxes were attached to the cabinet just above the washbasins.

二等舱肥皂盒
来源： 英国
年代： 爱德华时期，1912 年
尺寸： 12.22 厘米 x 7.46 厘米 x 5.71 厘米

Second Class Soap box
Origin: United Kingdom
Period: Edwardian Period, 1912
Size: 12.22 cm x 7.46 cm x 5.71 cm

从沉船遗址中打捞上来了十多个牙膏盒。这表明，白星航运可能为泰坦尼克号乘客免费提供这个品牌的洗浴用品。该产品由伦敦的约翰戈斯内尔有限公司 (John Gosnell &Co.,Ltd) 制造，是他们销售最好的品牌之一。牙膏盖上年轻的维多利亚女王的头像说明女王光顾过该公司。

Over a dozen of these toothpaste jars have been recovered from the wreck site suggesting that the White Star Line may have provided this brand to passengers traveling on *Titanic* as a complimentary toiletry item. The product was created by John Gosnell & Co., Ltd, London and was one of their most popular brands. The profile of a young Queen Victoria on the lid shows that the company was patronized by the Queen.

自动安全剃须刀片包装

来源： 英国
年代： 爱德华时期，1912 年
尺寸： 3.97 厘米 x 1.90 厘米

Auto Strop Safety Razor Blade Wrapper

Origin: United Kingdom
Period: Edwardian Period, 1912
Size: 3.97 cm x 1.90 cm

1912 年，许多男人使用拥有专利的安全剃刀剃胡须，有些人首选传统的直板剃刀，认为它更具男人味。起初，两家拥有专利的公司竞争安全剃刀的生意，一家是著名的吉列公司 (Gillette)，另一家是自动滑索安全剃刀公司 (Auto Strop Safety Razor)。最终，二家公司合并成为一家公司。

In 1912, many men shaved with the patented safety razor, while others still preferred the traditional straight razor, considering it more manly. Two companies that competed for the safety razor business were the well-known Gillette Company and the Auto Strop Safety

从沉船遗址中打捞上来一对旅行装肥皂盒。圆方形的盒子装有折页开关。

A couple of travel soap containers have been recovered from the wreck site. This rounded rectangular container has a hinged opening.

铜肥皂盒

来源： 英国
年代： 爱德华时期，1912 年
尺寸： 8.09 厘米 x 4.44 厘米 x 3.81 厘米

Copper Soap Box

Origin: United Kingdom
Period: Edwardian Period, 1912
Size: 8.09 cm x 4.44 cm x 3.81 cm

旅行剃须皂盒

来源： 美国
年代： 爱德华时期，1912 年
尺寸： 8.73 厘米 x 3.97 厘米

Shaving Soap Travel Case

Origin: United States
Period: Edwardian Period, 1912
Size: 8.73 cm x 3.97 cm

除非想蓄络腮胡，否则剃胡须被认为是男人日常打扮必不可少的一部分。由格拉斯顿伯里的康涅狄格州的 J. B. 威廉斯公司 (J. B. Williams Company of Glastonbury, Connecticut) 生产的剃须皂可能是最好的剃须皂之一。这件文物是当时非常流行的"威廉姆斯剃须棒"。

Unless sporting a full beard, shaving was considered an essential part of a man's daily grooming. Possibly one of the best shaving soaps every made was produced by the J. B. Williams Company of Glastonbury, Connecticut. This artifact is an example of the very popular "Williams Shaving Stick."

直式剃胡须刀柄

来源： 英国
年代： 爱德华时期，1912 年
尺寸： 13.97 厘米 x 1.59 厘米 x 0.79 厘米

Straight Razor Handle

Origin: United Kingdom
Period: Edwardian Period, 1912
Size: 13.97 cm x 1.59 cm x 0.79 cm

这种直式剃刀柄原来装有剃须钢刀片，用帆布或皮来磨刀。随着时间的推移，钢片被腐蚀了。

This straight razor handle originally held a steel blade used for shaving. The blade would have been sharpened using a strop, a canvas or leather strap. The steel has corroded over time.

特洛菲特 (H.P.Truefitt) 润发膏盒

来源： 英国
年代： 爱德华时期，1912 年
尺寸： 高 5.56 厘米；直径 7.94 厘米

H. P. Truefitt Hair Pomade Container

Origin:　United Kingdom
Period:　Edwardian Period, 1912
　Size:　h. 5.56 cm; diam. 7.94 cm

位于伦敦伯灵顿商的 H.P.TRUEFITT 是当时流行的美容产品供货商，包括紫罗兰等护发品。这个特殊的罐子用于装男式发蜡。如今，TRUEFITT & HILL 仍位于伦敦，继续制作天然香水等男士用品。

Located in the Burlington Arcade of London, H.P. TRUEFITT was a popular supplier of beauty products, including violet and melliflora scented preparations for hair. This particular jar held a pomade for men's hair. Today, Truefitt & Hill still located in London, continues to blend natural fragrances into their gentlemen's toiletries.

环把圆镜

来源： 法国
年代： 爱德华时期、1912 年
尺寸： 22.54 厘米 x 0.79 厘米 x 16.03 厘米

Circular Mirror with Loop Handle

Origin: France
Period: Edwardian Period, 1912
Size: 22.54 cm x 0.79 cm x 16.03 cm

在爱德华时期，仿象牙镜框、梳子和托盘是非常流行的洗漱用品。塑料在当时是新发明，制造商发现这种新材料只需花费一小部分成本就可以用来模仿象牙之类的奢侈品。这里展出的镜框由合成材料压制而成，标有"皇家科特迪瓦法国"字样。简化的手柄表明，它原本属于一套旅行梳妆用品。

Imitation ivory mirror frames, hairbrushes and trays were popular Edwardian toiletry items. Plastics were a recent invention and manufacturers found that the new substance could be used to imitate luxury wares like ivory at a fraction of the cost. This circular mirror frame is made of a synthetic material stamped "Royale Ivoire France." The reduced handle may indicate that it was originally part of a travel vanity set.

消遣活动
Pastime Activities

陶土烟管杆

来源： 欧洲
年代： 爱德华时期，1912 年
尺寸： 13.33 厘米 x 0.79 厘米

Partial Clay Pipe Stem

Origin: Europe
Period: Edwardian Period, 1912
Size: 13.33 cm x 0.79 cm

在爱德华时代男性社交圈中，吸烟和嚼烟都被看作时尚，但女性却不以为然。这根烟管展示了早期陶土烟管的风格。

Smoking and chewing tobacco was considered fashionable among men of Edwardian society, but frowned upon for women. This pipe stem fragment suggests an earlier clay pipe style.

黑皮折叠烟盒及 5 支烟
来源： 英国
年代： 爱德华时期，1912 年
尺寸： 8.89 厘米 x 7.94 厘米 x 2.54 厘米

Black Leather Folding Cigarette Case with Five Cigarettes

Origin: United Kingdom
Period: Edwardian Period, 1912
Size: 8.89 cm x 7.94 cm x 2.54 cm

8.89 cm x 7.94 cm x 2.54 cm

这个黑色的皮革折叠烟盒正面是金属框架和镀金装饰。里面装有 5 根土耳其和埃及的香烟。

This black leather folding cigarette case has a metal frame and gilded decoration on the front. The five Turkish and Egyptian cigarettes were found inside the case.

7.30 cm x 1.43 cm   7.62 cm x 1.43 cm

6.98 cm x 1.90 cm   7.94 cm x 1.90 cm   6.83 cm x 1.59 cm

3 张扑克牌

来源：美国
年代：爱德华时期，1912 年
尺寸：8.89 厘米 x 6.35 厘米（每张）

Three Playing Cards
Origin: United States
Period: Edwardian Period, 1912
Size: 8.89 cm x 6.35 cm (each)

这些名为"轮船 999"的扑克牌属于同一副扑克牌，发现于霍华德 • A. 欧文 (Howard A.Irwin) 的个人物品中。像这样的牌可能是用于坐船时玩的。许多头等舱绅士把玩纸牌看作一项令人愉快的社交消遣。然而，在泰坦尼克号上有几个"扑克老手"等待机会挑战那些天真的赌徒。史密斯 (Smith) 船长劝告有钱的乘客在坐下来赌博时小心这些老手，并指示手下在已知的"老手"想掏空其对手的钱包时，及时制止这种游戏。

These Steamboat 999 playing cards, part of an entire deck, were found among the personal effects of Howard A. Irwin. Cards like these were most likely used for playing poker while onboard. Many first-class gentlemen thought of card games as a pleasant social distraction. There were, however, several "card sharks" on *Titanic* waiting for an opportunity to challenge a naive gambler. Captain Smith advised his wealthy passengers to use caution when sitting down to gamble, and instructed his stewards to break up games in which a known "shark" was cleaning out his opponent's wallet.

81

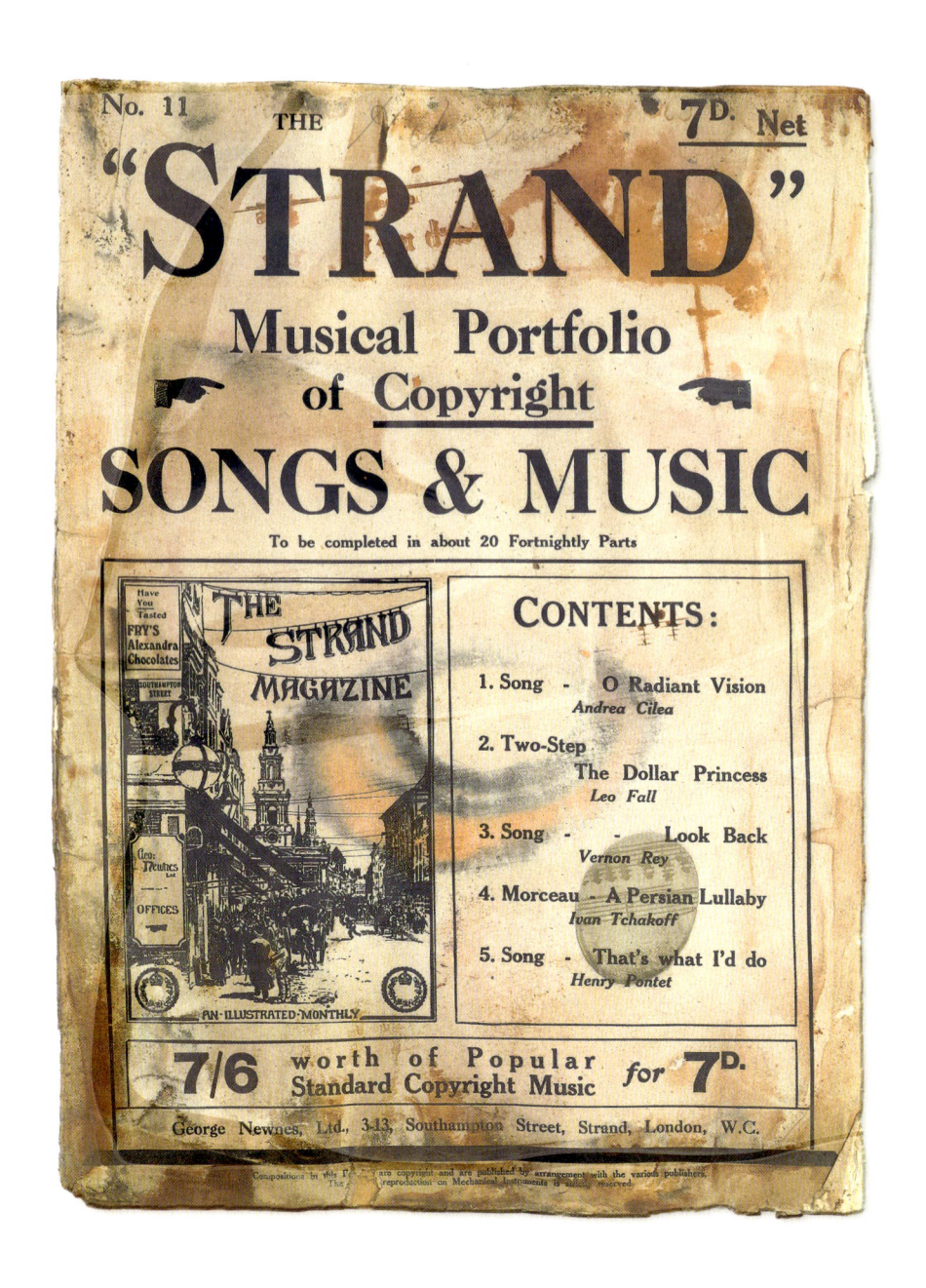

歌曲和音乐集

来源： 英国
年代： 爱德华时期，1910 年
尺寸： 35.56 厘米 x 26.19 厘米

Strand Musical Portfolio of Songs and Music

Origin: United Kingdom
Period: Edwardian Period, 1910
Size: 35.56 cm x 26.19 cm

20 多本乐谱小册子发现于霍华德·A. 欧文 (Howard A. Irwin) 的个人物品中，包括这本名为"歌曲和音乐集"的小册子。 这里面收集了 28 首 1910 年有版权的流行歌曲。

Over twenty booklets of sheet music were found among the personal effects of Howard A. Irwin, including this one entitled booklet " The Strand Musical Portfolio." It is a compilation of twenty-eight popular copyrighted songs in 1910.

茶壶

来源： 英国
年代： 爱德华时期，1912 年
尺寸： 高 12.38 厘米；壶口直径 8.57 厘米
壶体直径 45.72 厘米

Teapot

Origin: United Kingdom
Period: Edwardian Period, 1912
Size: h. 12.38 cm; rim diam. 8.57cm
body diam. 45.72 cm

这个坚固的褐色茶壶可能属于某位乘客。壶身上有 1 朵淡淡的金黄色花和藤蔓的图案。饮茶曾是一项全国性的消遣。

This sturdy brown teapot probably belonged to a passenger. It has a faint golden flower and vine design on the body. Drinking tea was a national pastime.

这一圆碗烟斗是"S"曲线形,意味着用嘴叼着烟斗时可以垂下来。斗钵壁和口柄用黄铜项圈连在一起。

This rounded bowl pipe has an "S" curve stem, means that it would have hung down from the mouth when held by the teeth. The bowl and stem are held together by a brass collar.

烟斗

来源: 英国
年代: 爱德华时期,1912 年
尺寸: 12.38 厘米 x 4.44 厘米 x 3.17 厘米

Rounded Bowl Pipe

Origin: United Kingdom
Period: Edwardian Period, 1912
Size: 12.38 cm x 4.44 cm x 3.17 cm

船上配置和家具

Ship Fittings and Furnitures

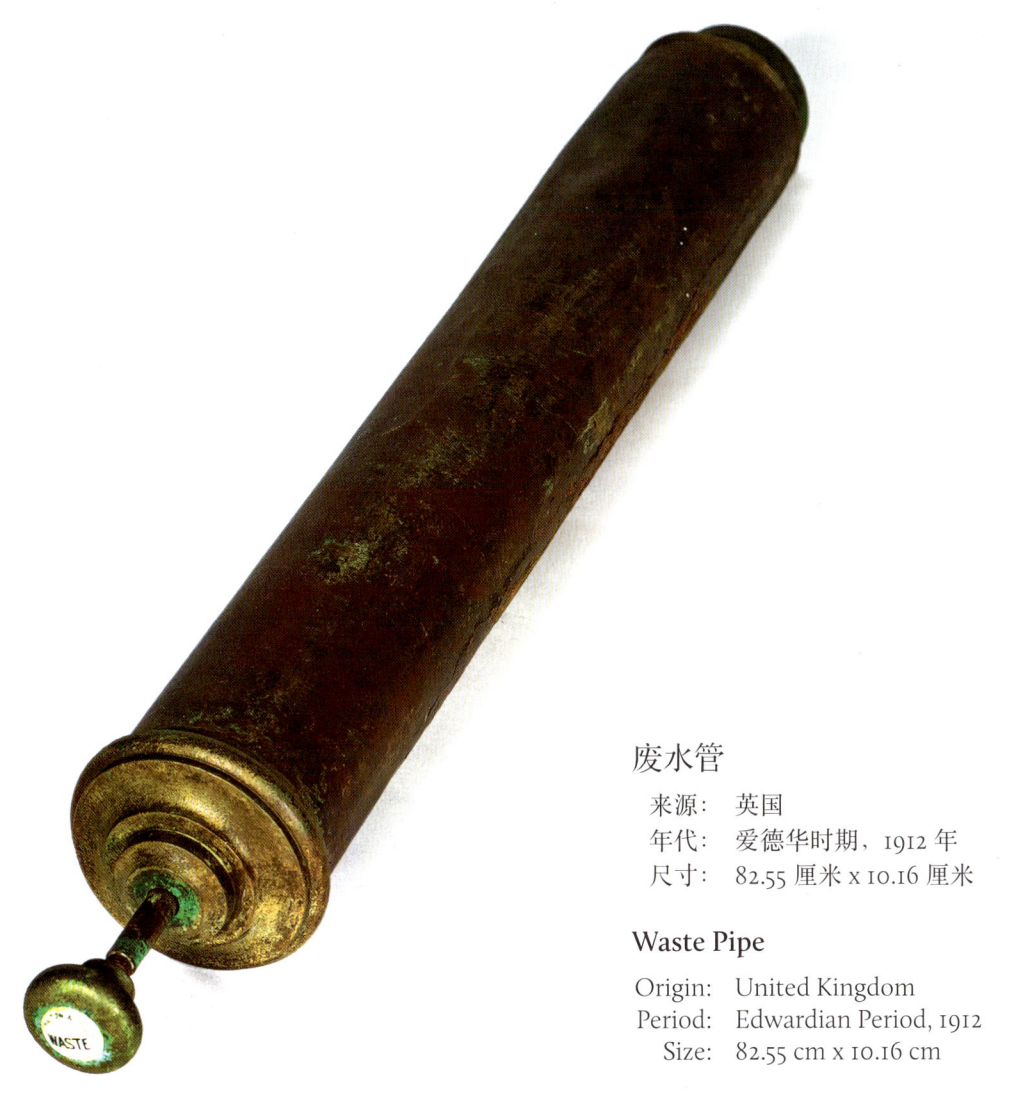

废水管

来源： 英国
年代： 爱德华时期，1912 年
尺寸： 82.55 厘米 x 10.16 厘米

Waste Pipe

Origin: United Kingdom
Period: Edwardian Period, 1912
Size: 82.55 cm x 10.16 cm

泰坦尼克号的浴缸底部没有排水塞。相反，他们有像这样镀镍的竖管。因为竖管被安装在浴缸的侧面，清洁工不必站在脏洗澡水里放水。

Bathtubs on *Titanic* did not have plugs in the bottom for drainage. Instead, they had nickel-plated standpipes like this one. Because the standpipes were placed at the side of the tub, clean bathers could drain the tub without reaching into the dirty bathwater for the stopper.

安装在大理石上的水龙头

来源： 英国
年代： 爱德华时期，1912 年
尺寸： 40.64 厘米 x 24.29 厘米 x 17.78 厘米

Faucet with Marble Surround

Origin: United Kingdom
Period: Edwardian Period, 1912
Size: 40.64 cm x 24.29 cm x 17.78 cm

只有头等舱船舱有自来水，二等舱和三等舱只好凑合着用洗脸盆。在头等舱私人浴室里，水槽周围装有大理石板挡水板。水龙头由 Shanks & Co., Ltd 有限公司制造，由弹簧自动关闭，防止在海上浪费宝贵的淡水。

Only first-class had running water in their cabins. Second and third class had to make do with washbasins. The marble slab formed a splash guard around the sink in a private, first-class bathroom. The tap, made by Shanks & Co., Ltd., is spring-loaded to shut automatically and prevent wasting precious fresh water at sea.

金边洗手盆

来源：英国
年代：爱德华时期、1912 年
尺寸：38.1 厘米 x 36.51 厘米 x 13.49 厘米

Porcelain Tip Sink

Origin: United Kingdom
Period: Edwardian Period, 1912
　Size: 38.1 cm x 36.51 cm x 13.49 cm

只有头等舱装有自来水。水箱隐藏在木柜子里，给二等舱洗手盆供水。洗完后，乘客把洗手盆折叠后收入墙壁以节省空间。用过的水流入第二个水箱，然后被工人清走。

Only first class cabins were fitted with running water. A tank hidden in a wooden cabinet fed this second class tip sink. When finished washing, passengers folded this sink into the wall to save space. The used water in the sink drained into a second tank, which was later emptied by a steward.

甲板灯

来源： 英国
年代： 爱德华时期，1912 年
尺寸： 10.48 厘米 x 23.49 厘米

Partial Deck Lamp

Origin: United Kingdom
Period: Edwardian Period, 1912
Size: 10.48 cm x 23.49 cm

甲板灯或牡蛎灯是用来照亮泰坦尼克号上层甲板的电灯。它们通过3个脚安装在墙上或天花板上。许多灯装有金属罩，防止强光干扰指挥桥台船员的夜间视力。玻璃盖和灯泡丢失。

Deck or oyster lamps were electrical lamps used to light *Titanic's* upper decks. They could be mounted by the three "feet" on a wall or ceiling. Many were fitted with metal screens to prevent their bright lights from impairing the Bridge Officer's night vision. The cover glass and lightbulb are missing.

应急舱电报铃

来源： 英国
年代： 爱德华时期，1912 年
尺寸： 高 6.35 厘米；直径 15.08 厘米

Emergency Engine Room Telegraph Bell

Origin: United Kingdom
Period: Edwardian Period, 1912
 Size: h. 6.35 cm; diam. 15.08 cm

铃也可称为锣，是应急机房电报机的一部分。指挥桥台的指令发送到机房，铃声就会响。

Bell can also be called gong, this bell was part of the Emergency Engine Room Telegraph. The bell sounded in response to instructions sent to the Engine Room from the Bridge.

地板砖

来源： 英国
年代： 爱德华时期，1912 年
尺寸： 15.24 厘米 x 15.24 厘米 x 1.59 厘米

Galley Floor Tile

Origin: United Kingdom
Period: Edwardian Period, 1912
Size: 15.24 cm x 15.24 cm x 1.59 cm

由 J. C. 爱德华兹 (J. C. Edwards) 制造，船上厨房使用的这种地砖有深槽，防止船员滑倒。背面印有制造商的名字，这种砖以耐磨损而出名。

This floor tile which was manufactured by J. C. Edwards, from the Ship's galleys have deep grooves to prevent crew members from slipping. Stamped with the maker's name on the back, these tiles were well known for their resistance to wear and tear.

整个船上都安装有这种青铜衣帽钩，用4个螺丝钉将其固定在墙上。爱德华时代的服饰标准包括西服和夹克，因此在泰坦尼克号上的所有客舱里都安装了衣帽钩。

Secured to walls by four screws, these bronze coat hooks were positioned throughout the Ship. The standard of dress in the Edwardian period included suits and jackets, hence the need for coat hooks in all service classes on *Titanic*.

衣帽钩

来源： 英国
年代： 爱德华时期，1912 年
尺寸： 6.19 厘米 x 7.93 厘米 x 2.22 厘米

Coat Hooks

Origin: United Kingdom
Period: Edwardian Period, 1912
Size: 6.19 cm x 7.93 cm x 2.22 cm

万向灯

来源： 英国
年代： 爱德华时期，1912 年
尺寸： 26.98 厘米 x 13.97 厘米

Gimbal Lamp in Two Pieces

Origin: United Kingdom
Period: Edwardian Period, 1912
Size: 26.98 cm x 13.97 cm

加固支点确保黄铜万向灯在任何天气情况下都保持直立。这盏灯原来是镀银的，加固支点现在分离了。这盏灯可以放在桌子上，也可以通过底座上的小环固定在墙上。

A weighted pivot ensured that this brass gimbal lamp would remain upright in any weather. The lamp was originally silver-plated, and the weighted pivot is now detached. The lamp could either be placed on a table or attached to a wall by an eye cast into its base.

水龙头

来源： 英国
年代： 爱德华时期，1912 年
尺寸： 13.65 厘米 x 4.60 厘米 x 10.00 厘米

Water tap
Origin: 　United Kingdom
Period: 　Edwardian Period, 1912
　Size: 　13.65 cm x 4.60 cm x 10.00 cm

泰坦尼克号上的二等舱并没有安装自来水。每天早晨，乘务员进入二等舱，重新装满红木柜里的储水箱。填充漏斗和储水箱相连，用来装水。洗手池的水来自储水箱，乘客在水池里洗漱，然后把水池折叠，塞进墙里，以节省空间。用过的水从水池排入第 2 个储水箱，然后由乘务员清空。此管和一个漏斗相连，用来给储水箱装水。

Second class cabins were not fitted with running water. Each morning, stewards entered second-class cabins to refill the reservoir water tank, which was hidden in a mahogany cabinet. A filling funnel was attached to the tank to assist with this process. The tank fed into a tip sink. Passengers washed from the sink, which then folded into the wall to save space. The used water remaining in the sink drained into a second tank, which a steward later emptied. This pipe had a funnel attached to it so that the reservoir could be filled.

机油配送箱

来源： 英国
年代： 爱德华时期，1912 年
尺寸： 39.37 厘米 x 23.17 厘米 x 15.87 厘米

Oil Distribution Box

Origin: United Kingdom
Period: Edwardian Period, 1912
Size: 39.37 cm x 23.17 cm x 15.87 cm

这件青铜色的文物是一个有盖的盒子，是发动机部件，负责给发动加机油，以防发动机因摩擦而损坏。

This bronze artifact is a compartmentalized box with hinged lid and dispensing apparatus designed to apply oil to moving parts of reciprocating engines at an optimal rate to prevent friction.

污水泵顶盖

来源： 英国
年代： 爱德华时期，1912 年
尺寸： 长 15.24 厘米

Waste Pump Knob

Origin: United Kingdom
Period: Edwardian Period, 1912
Size: l. 15.24cm

泰坦尼克号的浴缸底部没有排水塞。相反，他们有由道尔顿公司（Doulton & Company）生产的镀镍竖管和活塞旋钮。因为竖管被安装在浴缸的侧面，所以清洁工不必站在脏洗澡水里放水。

There's no drain plug at the bottom of *Titanic's* bathtub. Instead, they had nickel-plated standpipes and plunger knobs made by Doulton & Company. Because the standpipes were placed at the side of the tub, clean bathers could drain the tub without reaching into the dirty bathwater for the stopper.

冷热水龙头

来源： 英国
年代： 爱德华时期，1912 年
尺寸： 26.98 厘米 x 8.25 厘米 x 24.76 厘米

Hot and Cold Water Faucets

Origin:　United Kingdom
Period:　Edwardian Period, 1912
Size:　　26.98 cm x 8.25 cm x 24.76 cm

这套冷热海水水龙头用于泰坦尼克号浴缸。海水泡澡被认为有治疗作用，同时还提供一种特殊的起泡盐肥皂。在洗澡结束时，乘客用淡水洗去海水。这套水龙头由道尔顿公司 (Doulton&Company) 制造，阀门的标签是瓷制的。

This set of valves filled *Titanic's* bathtubs with hot and cold seawater. Bathing in ocean water was considered therapeutic, and a special salt-lathering soap was provided for washing. At the end of the bath, passengers washed away seawater with fresh water. This set of water faucets was made by Doulton & Company, the valve labels are of porcelain.

1912 年，有关救生艇搭载量的法律已过时。法规荒唐的规定，救生艇的数量取决于船舶的尺寸，而不是船上的实际人数。泰坦尼克号的木制救生艇由起重机的钢吊艇架（Welin davits）吊起后，再用麻绳放到水里。当救生艇放入水中时，用控制支架和滑轮的角度来防止绳子滑落。

In 1912, the laws governing lifeboat capacity were hopelessly outdated. Through a quirk in the regulations, the number of lifeboats depended on the physical size of the Ship, not the actual number of persons onboard. *Titanic's* wooden lifeboats were lowered to the water on hemp ropes by means of steel cranes called Welin davits. This angle bracket and wheel is part of a guide that prevented the ropes from becoming entangled with each other as the boat was lowered.

双吊艇架铁滑轮

来源： 英国
年代： 爱德华时期，1912 年
尺寸： 75.56 厘米 x 31.27 厘米

Welin Davit Pulley

Origin: United Kingdom
Period: Edwardian Period, 1912
Size: 75.56 cm x 31.27 cm

唯宝梅特拉赫 (Villeroy & Boch Mettach) 瓷砖

来源： 欧洲
年代： 爱德华时期、1912 年
尺寸： ① 16.98 厘米 x 16.98 厘米 x 1.90 厘米
　　　② 6.82 厘米 x 6.82 厘米 x 1.58 厘米
　　　③ 16.98 厘米 x 16.82 厘米 x 1.74 厘米

Villeroy & Boch Mettlach Ceramic Tiles

Origin: Europe
Period: Edwardian Period, 1912
Size: ① 16.98 cm x 16.98 cm x 1.90 cm
　　　② 6.82 cm x 6.82 cm x 1.58 cm
　　　③ 16.98 cm x 16.82 cm x 1.74 cm

①

②

大部分泰坦尼克号头等舱和二等舱的厕所、土耳其浴室以及游泳池四壁都使用这种唯宝梅特拉赫 (Villeroy & Boch Mettach) 瓷砖。瓷砖的仿马赛克表面纹理是为了增加摩擦力和防滑，这种瓷砖的图案为八角形和正方形。

Most of *Titanic's* first and second class lavatories, the Turkish Bathroom, and the swimming pool surround used this Villeroy & Boch Mettlach ceramic tiles. The faux-mosaic surface treatment of the tile provided traction and prevented slipping. The encaustic tiles created a pattern of octagons and squares.

③

装饰用木家具组件

来源： 英国
年代： 爱德华时期、1912 年
尺寸： 15.87 厘米 x 3.65 厘米 x 4.28 厘米

Decorative Wooden Furniture Element

Origin: United Kingdom
Period: Edwardian Period, 1912
Size: 15.87 cm x 3.65 cm x 4.28 cm

从泰坦尼克号打捞上来的木制文物极少。从历史照片来看，这件文物可能是头等舱餐厅的家具部件。

Few wooden artifacts have been recovered from *Titanic*. Based upon historic photographs, this may be an element from the First Class Dining Saloon.

气缸指示器
来源： 英国
年代： 爱德华时期，1912 年
尺寸： 23.81 厘米 x 22.22 厘米 x 11.43 厘米

Wood Box with Steam Engine Indicator
Origin:　United Kingdom
Period:　Edwardian Period, 1912
　Size:　23.81 cm x 22.22 cm x 11.43 cm

这个设备用于测量船的马力，使用时临时将其连接到泰坦尼克号的发动机气缸上。类似于地震仪的笔，标记触笔根据气缸运动画出楔形图。船舶工程师通过图形了解泰坦尼克号的运行阀门运作是否有异常。这是白星航运的设备，由工程师进行维护。

This device was used to measure the Ship's horse power, when temporarily attached to the cylinders of *Titanic*'s engines. Similar to the pen on a seismograph, a marking stylus responded to the cylinders' movement, drawing a wedge-shaped diagram. The Ship's engineers studied this diagram for irregularities in *Titanic*'s valve settings. This was White Star Line equipment and would have been kept by the engineers.

镀金吊灯

来源： 英国
年代： 爱德华时期，1912 年
尺寸： 2.22 厘米 x 30.48 厘米

Chandelier

Origin: United Kingdom
Period: Edwardian Period, 1912
Size: 2.22 cm x 30.48 cm

这盏镀金吊灯是大楼梯门厅灯之一。它有用切割玻璃球体（现已下落不明）代替棱镜，表明它安装在下层甲板。花位于球体的底部，三只灯泡放在球体内部。

This gilded chandelier is from one of the Grand Staircase foyers. It had a cut-glass globe (now missing) instead of prisms, indicating it comes from one of the lower decks. The flower would have been at the bottom of the globe, three light bulbs were inside the globe.

三等舱地砖

来源： 英国
年代： 爱德华时期、1912 年
尺寸： 16.82 厘米 x 16.82 厘米 x 1.74 厘米

Third Class Floor Tile

Origin: United Kingdom
Period: Edwardian Period, 1912
Size: 16.82 cm x 16.82 cm x 1.74 cm

船员舱和三等舱的厕所和浴室大都镶嵌这种马赛克风格图案的黑白相间的瓷砖，这种白圆圈里黑色四角星的地砖由唯宝梅特拉赫 (Villeroy & Boch Mettlach) 设计制造。

Many crew and third class lavatories and bathrooms featured these serviceable encaustic, mosaic style pattern black and white tiles. The design is a four-pointed black star in a white circle and made by Villeroy & Boch Mettlach.

扶手支架

来源： 英国
年代： 爱德华时期，1912 年
尺寸： 10.63 厘米 x 4.28 厘米；9.05 厘米 x 4.13 厘米

Handrail Brackets

Origin: United Kingdom
Period: Edwardian Period, 1912
　Size: 10.63 cm x 4.28 cm; 9.05 cm x 4.13 cm

整个泰坦尼克号上到处都是木制栏杆。这些栏杆的支架由铜合金制成，用于连接扶手。

Wooden handrails were located throughout all areas of the *Titanic*. These brackets, made of copper alloy, were used to connect handrail.

陶瓷灯盖

来源： 英国
年代： 爱德华时期，1912 年
尺寸： 6.35 厘米 x 10.79 厘米

Porcelain Light Cover

Origin: United Kingdom
Period: Edwardian Period, 1912
Size: 6.35 cm x 10.79 cm

这是一种新艺术风格的设计，表面呈波浪形并刻有树叶纹路。设计这种陶瓷盖用于隐藏电源插座，这些固定装置被安装在二等舱和三等舱的天花板上。

This is an Art Nouveau style design, with a wavy surface and leaf texture. This porcelain cover was used to hide the electrical socket for a single, ceiling-mounted, light bulb. These fixtures were used in second and third class accommodations.

装饰砖

来源： 英国
年代： 爱德华时期，1912 年
尺寸： 14.44 厘米 x 14.60 厘米 x 0.47 厘米

Decorative Tile

Origin: United Kingdom
Period: Edwardian Period, 1912
　Size: 14.44 cm x 14.60 cm x 0.47 cm

这里展示的红色和白色的鸢尾花地砖，用于二等舱和三等舱的公共区域。安装时拼成白底红花，或者红底白花图案。这种瓷砖也可用于大面积区域的边界装饰。

Red and white fleur-de-lis floor tiles displayed here, were used in second and third class public spaces. They were installed in an alternating patter of red on white, and white on red. These tiles could be used with a border in larger areas.

105

20 安培拇指保险丝

来源： 英国
年代： 爱德华时期、1912 年
尺寸： 10.16 厘米 x 5.71 厘米 x 2.54 厘米

20 Amp Thumb Fuse

Origin:　United Kingdom
Period:　Edwardian Period, 1912
 Size:　10.16 cm x 5.71 cm x 2.54 cm

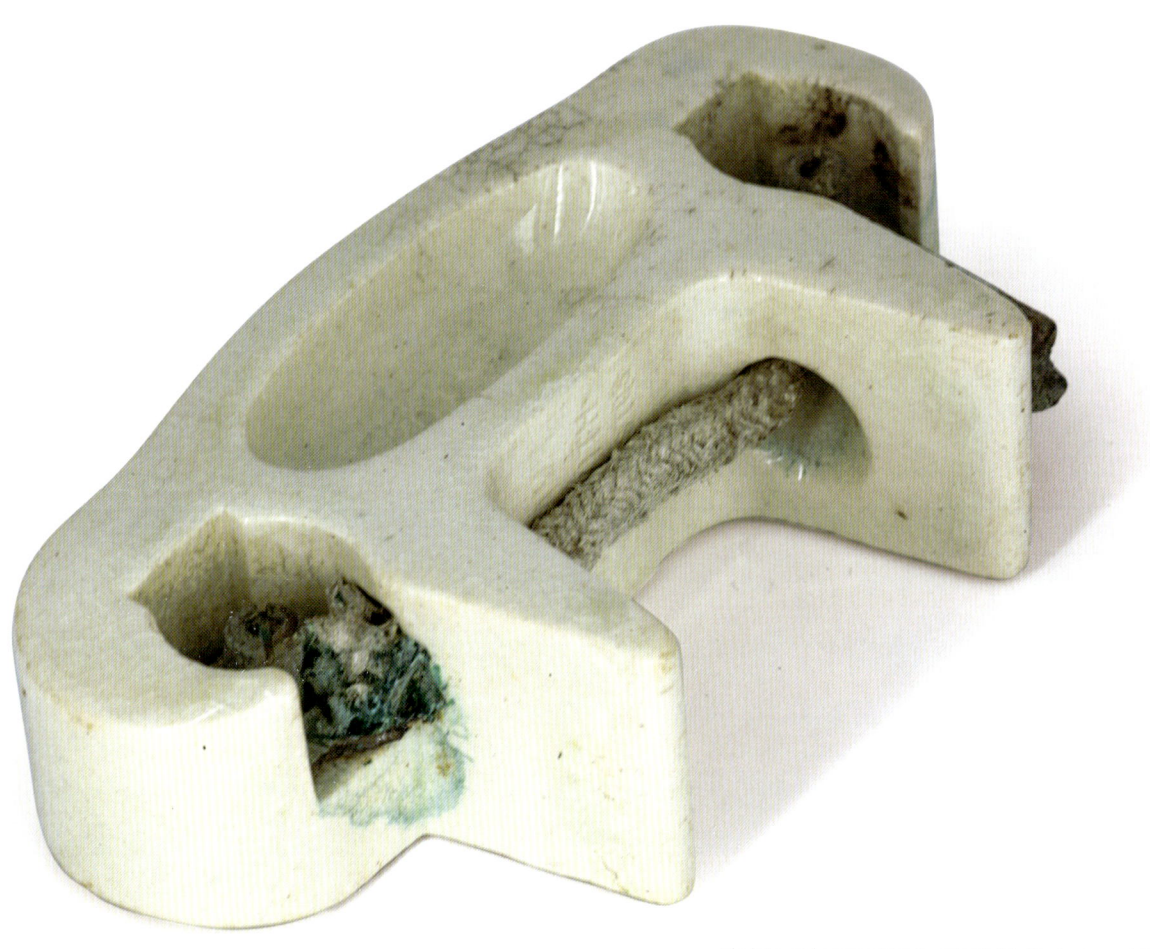

泰坦尼克号可以为整船提供电力。这是一个 20 安培的陶制保险丝盒，侧面配有手指握柱，中间的间隔架可以防止保险丝被溶解。

Titanic provide electricity for all the Ship. This is a 20 amp frame from a fuse box. It is of fired earthenware, cast with finger grips on the side, and features spacer legs to prevent crushing the fusible.

甲板灯

来源： 英国
年代： 爱德华时期，1912 年
尺寸： 36.19 厘米 x 32.06 厘米 x 10.16 厘米

Deck Light

Origin:　United Kingdom
Period:　Edwardian Period, 1912
　Size:　36.19 cm x 32.06 cm x 10.16 cm

这个青铜制的甲板灯是由伦敦海伍德兄弟公司 (Haywood Brothers of London) 制造，它由一系列安装在甲板的黄铜框架里的棱镜组成。其目的是捕捉和驱散周围的太阳光，最大程度地提供照明，以便工程师修理头等舱电梯的机件。

This artifact is a bronze deck light made by the Haywood Brothers of London. It consists of a series of prisms held in a brass frame that was installed in the deck. The purpose was to catch and disperse ambient sun light to prove maximum illumination so that engineers could make repairs on the first class elevator machinery.

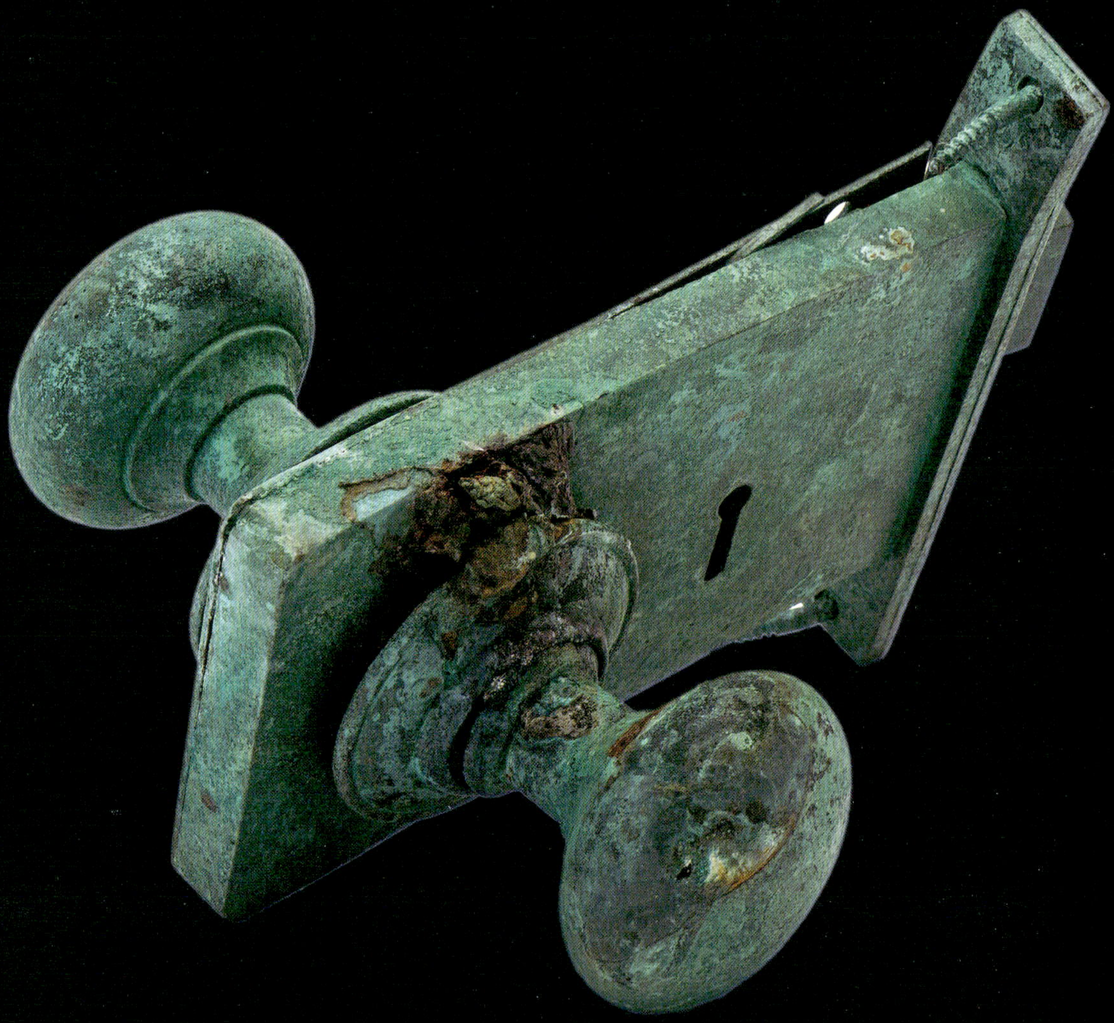

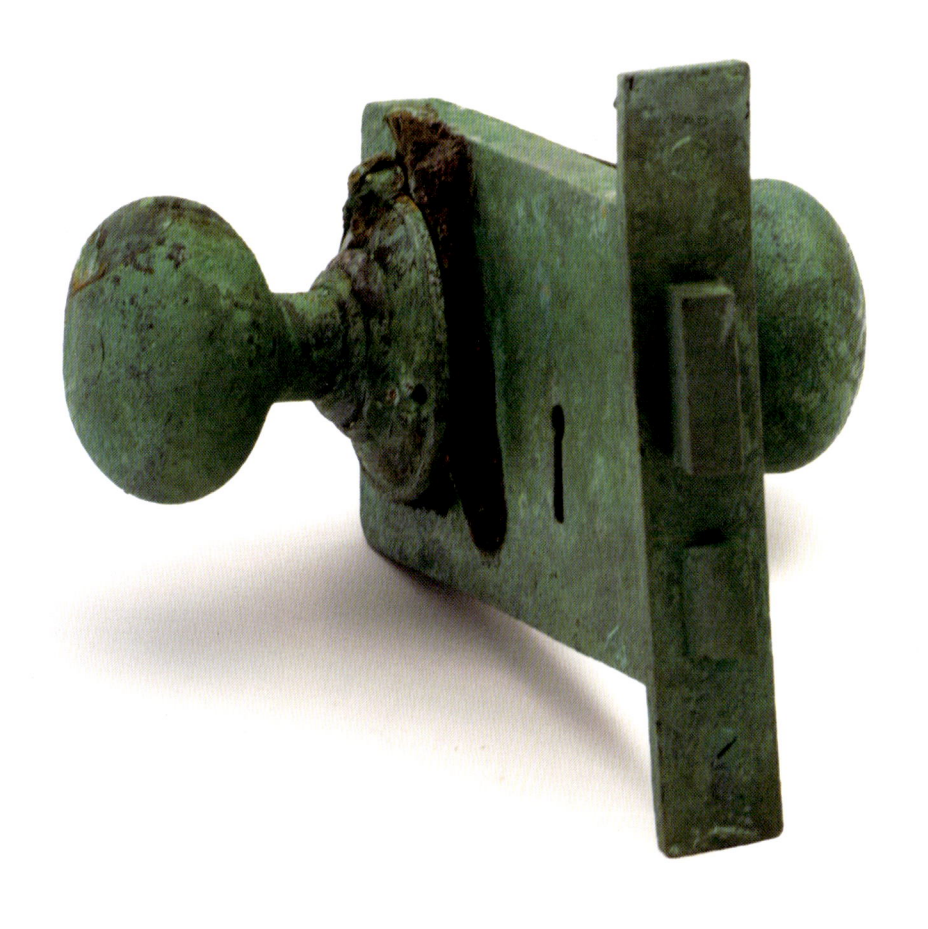

镶木暗锁

来源： 英国
年代： 爱德华时期，1912 年
尺寸： 15.24 厘米 x 15.24 厘米 x 13.97 厘米

Mortice Lock with Door Knobs

Origin: United Kingdom
Period: Edwardian Period, 1912
Size: 15.24 cm x 15.24 cm x 13.97 cm

安装暗锁需要木匠技术，以确保锁被准确地安装到门里。门两侧都有把手和钥匙孔，它可能是用来进入船舱的。

Installing this mortice lock required the skills of a carpenter to ensure that it was fitted cleanly into a door. There are door knobs on both sides and a key hole for locking the dead bolt. It was probably used to access a cabin.

壁灯

来源： 英国
年代： 爱德华时期，1912 年
尺寸： 25.4 厘米 x 15.24 厘米 x 60.96 厘米

Wall Sconce

Origin: United Kingdom
Period: Edwardian Period, 1912
Size: 25.4 cm x 15.24 cm x 60.96 cm

这种 3 个球状镀金壁灯位于头等舱 Á la Carte 餐厅。它的上半部分是花卉装饰，底部是蛇缠绕图案。

This three-bulb gilded wall sconce was located in the First Class Á la Carte Restaurant. It shows a floral decoration on the upper half and an entwined serpent motif at the bottom.

旋转梯栏杆的装饰花环

来源： 英国
年代： 爱德华时期，1912 年
尺寸： 34.29 厘米 x 7.62 厘米 x 1.27 厘米

Decorative Garland Section of Grand Staircase Balustrade

Origin: United Kingdom
Period: Edwardian Period, 1912
Size: 34.29 cm x 7.62 cm x 1.27 cm

泰坦尼克号的大楼梯是头等舱乘客喜爱的聚会场所。每一级楼梯都有镶嵌木和镀金装饰，如青铜色的天使，为上面的台阶增色不少。这种镀金金属装饰花环主要用于装饰头等舱楼梯的黑色铁栏杆。

Titanic's Grand Staircase was a favorite meeting place for first class passengers. Each level of the staircase was adorned with inlaid wood and gilded ornaments, such as a bronze cherub that graced one of the upper landings. This gilt metal garland embellished the black wrought-iron banisters of the main First Class Staircase.

煤

来源： 英国
年代： 爱德华时期，1912 年
尺寸： 30.48 厘米 x 26.67 厘米 x 16.51 厘米

Coal

Origin:　United Kingdom
Period:　Edwardian Period, 1912
　Size:　30.48 cm x 26.67 cm x 16.51 cm

泰坦尼克号离开英国时装载了 6000 吨煤，这些煤既为船上锅炉提供动力，又用于厨房做饭。船上的煤大多是从因煤矿工人罢工而被迫取消航行的小船上购买而来。泰坦尼克号每航行 1 米，就要消耗 1.5 千克煤，所以 30 千克煤块可以供船航行约 20 米，或让船全速前进约 1.5 秒。

Titanic left England carrying 6,000 tons of coal, these are both to power the Ship's vast boilers and for cooking in her galleys. Much of the coal was taken from smaller ships whose sailings were canceled due to a miners' strike. *Titanic* consumed 1.5 kilograms of coal for every meter (1 pound per foot) travelled, therefore a 30kg lump could move the Ship through the water about 20 meters, or about 1.5 seconds at full speed.

餐饮服务、设备和装饰
Dining Service, Equipment and Decorations

头等舱服务
First Class Service

头等舱茶碟
来源： 英国
年代： 爱德华时期，1912 年
尺寸： 2.54 厘米 x 13.81 厘米

First-Class Tea Saucer
Origin: United Kingdom
Period: Edwardian Period, 1912
Size: 2.54 cm x 13.81 cm

生产商在茶碟背面标注的生产日期是 1911 年 3 月，从时间上看正是在泰坦尼克号的姐妹船——奥林匹克的首航期间。当时，白星航运公司为了节省成本，购买了足够两条船使用的瓷器。碟子虽有浸渍，但依然可见棕色和青绿色的"格状"图案。

The maker's marks on the reverse side of this saucer give its date of manufacture as March 1911, in time for the maiden voyage of *Titanic's* sister ship, *Olympic*. White Star Line ordered the production of enough china to outfit both ships as a cost-saving measure. The decorative design, damaged from immersion is often referred to as the "trellis'" pattern in brown and turquoise.

113

头等舱饮水器

来源： 英国
年代： 爱德华时期，1912 年
尺寸： 21.75 厘米 x 13.65 厘米

First Class Water Decanter

Origin:　　United Kingdom
Period:　　Edwardian Period, 1912
　Size:　　21.75 cm x 13.65 cm

虽然泰坦尼克号的某些船舱里有自来水,乘客却不能饮用船舱里的自来水。而在船舱和公共区域,乘务员提供配有盛装饮用水的玻璃瓶,上面刻有白星航运标志,不同等级的船舱使用的水瓶玻璃质量不同。

Although some of *Titanic's* cabins had running water, passengers could not drink the Ship's tap water. Instead, stewards supplied drinking water in decanters etched with the White Star flag which were found in cabins and public rooms. The quality of the glass used varied depending upon the class for which it was intended.

①

②

蛋 杯

来源： 英国
年代： 爱德华时期，1912 年
尺寸： ① 6.67 厘米 x 4.60 厘米
② 5.87 厘米 x 5.56 厘米

Egg Cups

Origin: United Kingdom, Europe
Period: Edwardian Period, 1912
Size: ① 6.67 cm x 4.60 cm
② 5.87 cm x 5.56 cm

蛋杯可用于盛装单只水煮鸡蛋。上面这个蛋杯用于头等舱餐厅，左边这个蛋杯上装饰着一只母鸡图案的贴花，表明它属于某位乘客。

Eggcups were used to serve a single soft-boiled egg. This egg cup is from the First Class Dining Saloon. Another cup features the remains of a running hen decal, indicating that it belonged to a passenger.

三叶开胃小菜盘

来源: 英国
年代: 爱德华时期,1912 年
尺寸: 5.56 厘米 x 26.36 厘米

Trefoil Appetizer Serving Dish

Origin: United Kingdom
Period: Edwardian Period, 1912
Size: 5.56 cm x 26.36 cm

这个盛装开胃菜的菜碟用于头等舱的接待厅和餐厅。碟子底部有 3 个孔,以便服务员为顾客上菜时能很舒适地抓住它。碟子上的手绘装饰已经看不见了。

This serving dish was used in the First Class Reception and Dining Saloon to pass appetizers. At the base of dish has three holes so that the server could hold the plate comfortably while serving guests. The hand painted decoration on the dish is no longer visible.

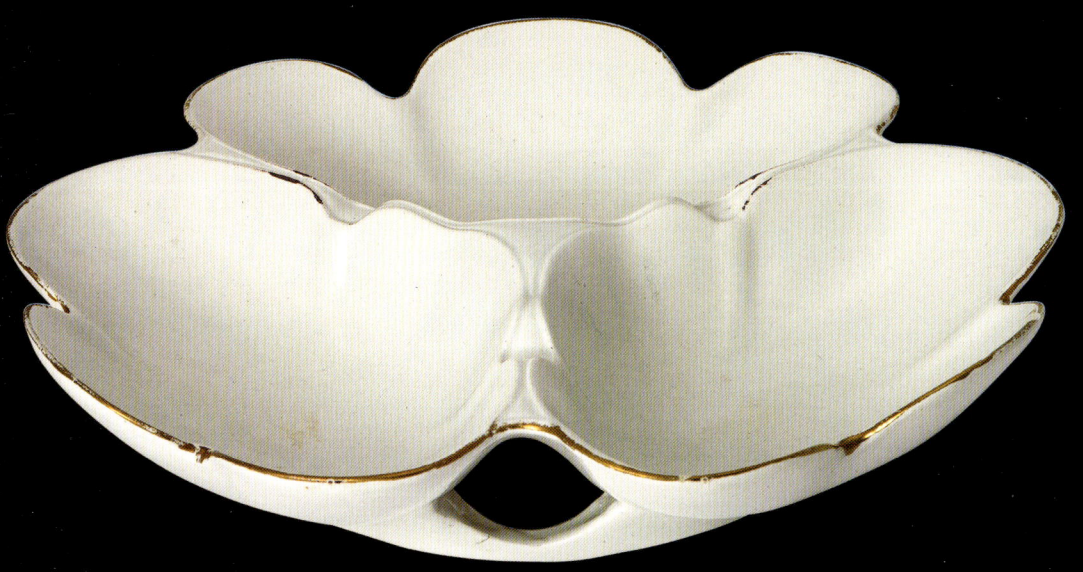

银碟盖

来源： 英国
年代： 爱德华时期，1912 年
尺寸： 27.62 厘米 x 4.13 厘米

Silver Plated Serving Dish Lid

Origin: United Kingdom
Period: Edwardian Period, 1912
Size: 27.62 cm x 4.13 cm

带盖子的餐具在食物从厨房送到餐桌的过程中可以保持食品温度。服务员将食品送到用餐者面前时，再掀开盖子。这个用于头等舱餐厅的银盘盖很可能是用来盛装芦笋的，因为食用芦笋在爱德华时代风靡一时。

Serving dishes with lids were used to ensure the food was kept hot in transit from galley to table. The lid would then be lifted, and the food "presented" to the diner. This First Class Dining Saloon lid was most likely used for serving asparagus, as that vegetable was all the rage in Edwardian society.

冰黄油镀银盘

来源： 英国
年代： 爱德华时期，1912 年
尺寸： 4.44 厘米 x 17.78 厘米

Silver Plated Iced Butter Dish

Origin: United Kingdom
Period: Edwardian Period, 1912
Size: 4.44 cm x 17.78 cm

从沉船处打捞上来 17 件这种银盘。研究表明，这套镀银底的盘子是用来盛装冰镇黄油的。在盘子的底部铺上碎冰，上面盖上 1 个穿孔的托盘，用于冷藏黄油。盘子由埃尔金顿 (Elkington) 公司制作。

A stack of seventeen of these dishes were recovered from the wreck site. Research indicates that they are the silver plated bases for an iced butter dish. Crushed ice in the bottom would have been covered by a pierced tray to keep butter cold. The dishes were made by Elkington Plate.

甲板上用的杯碟

来源： 英国
年代： 爱德华时期，1912 年
尺寸： 6.83 厘米 x 10.32 厘米

Cup and Saucer from Deck Servicer

Origin: United Kingdom
Period: Edwardian Period, 1912
Size: 6.83 cm x 10.32 cm

这只超大杯子用来盛装肉汤和热巧克力，供坐在甲板上的头等舱乘客享用。

This oversized cup was used to serve bouillon and hot chocolate to first-class passengers seated in lounge chairs on deck.

这种用于头等舱餐厅的勺子原本是镀银的，椭圆形，手柄前端有个星形图案。

Originally silver plated, this ladle was used in the First Class Restaurant. The bowl is oval and there is a star at the tip of the handle.

头等舱餐厅勺子

来源： 英国
年代： 爱德华时期，1912 年
尺寸： 31.75 厘米 x 9.84 厘米 x 6.82 厘米

Ladle from First Class Restaurant

Origin: United Kingdom
Period: Edwardian Period, 1912
Size: 31.75 cm x 9.84 cm x 6.82 cm

茶匙和调味叉

来源： 英国
年代： 爱德华时期，1912 年
尺寸： ① 12.7 厘米 x 2.54 厘米 x 1.11 厘米
② 15.39 厘米 x 1.74 厘米 x 0.95 厘米

Teaspoon and Relish Fork

Origin:　United Kingdom
Period:　Edwardian Period, 1912
　Size:　① 12.7 cm x 2.54 cm x 1.11 cm
② 15.39 cm x 1.74 cm x 0.95 cm

①

头等舱餐厅里的餐具通常都是镀银的。这个茶匙头内部是镀金的，茶柄的前端有 1 个星形图案。调味叉用于调食品的味道，波浪齿的设计让食品的味道更好地融合在一起，也会让盘中食物的液体流走。叉柄的前端也有 1 颗星形图案。

Cutlery in the First Class Dining Saloon was always silver plated. The teaspoon also has a gold wash on the bowl interior and a star at the tip of the handle. A relish fork was used to extract a small serving of relish or other condiments. The wavy tines are set close together to hold the condiment, allowing any liquid to drain before placing it on the plate. They also have a star on the tip of the handle.

②

头等舱 Á la Carte 餐厅小吃盘

来源： 英国
年代： 爱德华时期、1912 年
尺寸： 1.587 厘米 x 20.63 厘米

Side Plate from First Class Á la Carte Restaurant

Origin: United Kingdom
Period: Edwardian Period, 1912
Size: 1.587 cm x 20.63 cm

这只午宴用的小碟来自头等舱的 Á la Carte 餐厅。这家餐厅的特色是提供了比头等舱其他餐厅更为精致的菜单，在食物和服务标准方面的要求都是最高规格。乘客在这家餐厅用餐需要支付额外的费用，这些费用不包括在船票价格里。

原装饰是金镶边与新古典主义的花环图案交替。此外还有白星航运的正式徽标：胜利花环环绕着的 OSNC（海洋蒸汽航行公司）。

This luncheon side plate came from the exclusive Á la Carte Restaurant. The Restaurant featured a much more elaborate menu than the First Class Dining Saloon and maintained the highest standards in food and service. Passengers were required to pay an additional fee for this measure of service, as the extra cost was not covered in the price of the passage ticket.

Originally decorated with a gold band and neoclassic wreath pattern that alternated with garlands, it also had the formal monogram of the White Star Line: OSNC (Oceanic Steam Navigation Company) surrounded by a victory wreath.

特殊服务小咖啡杯和盘子碎片

来源： 英国
年代： 爱德华时期，1912 年
尺寸： 5.39 厘米 x 5.39 厘米
      12.54 厘米 x 5.39 厘米 x 0.79 厘米

Special Service Demitasse Cup and Partial Saucer

Origin: United Kingdom
Period: Edwardian Period, 1912
  Size: 5.39 cm x 5.39 cm
         12.54 cm x 5.39 cm x 0.79 cm

这种昂贵的钴蓝色与金色相间的瓷器，由斯波德瓷器有限公司 (Spode China Ltd.) 提供，头等舱精英乘客专用。在餐盘中间拼写着白星航运的正式名称的首写字母："海洋蒸汽航行公司"。这套杯盘被认为用于头等舱 Á la Carte 餐厅。

This expensive cobalt blue and gold porcelain china, provided by Spode China Ltd., was reserved for "elite" first class passengers. The interlocking letters in the middle of the dinner plate spell out the initials of the White Star Line's official name: "The Oceanic Steam Navigation Company." It is believed to be the dinner service for the First Class Restaurant.

巴黎咖啡厅小型咖啡杯

来源： 英国
年代： 爱德华时期，1912 年
尺寸： 5.39 厘米 x 5.23 厘米

Café Parisien Demitasse Cup

Origin: United Kingdom
Period: Edwardian Period, 1912
Size: 5.39 cm x 5.23 cm

根据咖啡杯口上昂贵的钴蓝和金边装饰推测，这个咖啡杯用于头等舱巴黎咖啡厅里。巴黎咖啡厅紧挨着 Á la Carte 高档餐厅。这个咖啡杯杯口的蓝色边突显金黄色希腊式设计。

The coffee cup is thought to be used in first-class café adjacent, based on the expensive cobalt blue and gold decorations on the clasp. Café Parisien is near to Á la Carte Restaurant. It features a blue rim band highlighted by a gold Greek key design.

这个贝壳形状的水晶盘由手工打磨制造,很可能用于头等舱。它的设计优雅、现代,底部刻有白星航运的商标。从沉船遗址中打捞了 8 个同样的盘子。

The difficult handmade cuts in this shell-shaped crystal dish indicate that it was probably used in First Class. It has an elegant, modern design with the White Star Line logo etched in the heel. Eight identical dishes were recovered from the wreck site.

头等舱甜点盘

来源: 英国
年代: 爱德华时期,1912 年
尺寸: 15.4 厘米 x 9.52 厘米 x 3.02 厘米

First Class Candy Dish

Origin: United Kingdom
Period: Edwardian Period, 1912
Size: 15.4 cm x 9.52 cm x 3.02 cm

二等舱服务
Second Class Service

二等舱水罐
来源： 英国
年代： 爱德华时期，1912 年
尺寸： 13.18 厘米 x 11.43 厘米

Second Class Pitcher
Origin: United Kingdom
Period: Edwardian Period, 1912
Size: 13.18 cm x 11.43 cm

在装饰上，模仿中国传统青花瓷器风格，这种独特的代尔夫特蓝瓷于 1871 年申请了专利，至今仍然流行。尽管这种装饰很受欢迎，但用于二等舱餐厅的瓷器的装饰的精细程度和品质远不如用于头等舱的瓷器。代尔夫特或荷兰蓝白色瓷器图案风格是在广东瓷器从中国运到欧洲后而形成的。

Decorated with traditional blue and white stylized flowers, this particular Blue Delft china pattern was registered in 1871, and has remained so popular that it is still available today. While still attractive, the refinement of decoration and quality of this restaurant grade china are inferior to that of the china used in First Class. The Delft or Holland blue and white wares were patterned after Canton porcelain wares shipped from China to Europe.

二等舱盘子

来源： 英国
年代： 爱德华时期，1912 年
尺寸： 3.02 厘米 x 24.76 厘米

Second Class Plates

Origin: United Kingdom
Period: Edwardian Period, 1912
  Size: 3.02 cm x 24.76 cm

这些餐馆级别的青花瓷器用于二等舱餐厅。

These restaurant grade blue and white china service pieces were used in the Second Class Dining Saloon.

二等舱碟子

来源： 英国
年代： 爱德华时期，1912 年
尺寸： 11.11 厘米 x 25.4 厘米

Second Class Dish

Origin: United Kingdom
Period: Edwardian Period, 1912
Size: 11.11 cm x 25.4 cm

这个镀银盘可能用于二等舱餐厅盛装水果，也可能用作中心装饰品。

This silver plated dish was probably used in the Second Class Dining Saloon to serve fruit. It may have also been served as a centerpiece.

三等舱服务
Third Class Service

三等舱汤盘
来源： 英国
年代： 爱德华时期，1912 年
尺寸： 4.13 厘米 x 23.65 厘米

Third Class Soup Plate
Origin: United Kingdom
Period: Edwardian Period, 1912
Size: 4.13 cm x 23.65 cm

三等舱餐厅汤盘，比较重，白色釉面，中心刻有白星航运的标志。如同船上的其他瓷器，瓷器上没有泰坦尼克号的名字，也可用在其他白星航运公司的船上。

Heavy and serviceable, the white glazed third class dining room earthenware was marked only with the White Star Line's logo at the center. Like all china onboard, the name *Titanic* never appeared, allowing its use on other White Star Line ships, if necessary.

三等舱水杯

来源： 英国
年代： 爱德华时期，1912 年
尺寸： 8.09 厘米 x 8.25 厘米

Third Class Mug

Origin: United Kingdom
Period: Edwardian Period, 1912
Size: 8.09 cm x 8.25 cm

这水杯符合三等舱的服务标准。这是从沉船遗址上打捞上来的唯一一件这种形状的杯子，可能是用来喝咖啡的。

This mug matches the standard of third class service. It is the only mug of this shape that has been recovered from the wreck site and was probably used for coffee.

三等舱水瓶

来源： 英国
年代： 爱德华时期，1912 年
尺寸： 22.54 厘米 x 11.11 厘米

Third Class Water Carafe

Origin: United Kingdom
Period: Edwardian Period, 1912
Size: 22.54 cm x 11.11 cm

因其有限的装饰，可以确定这种大水瓶用于三等舱。这种大水瓶被放在公共区和餐饮区，为所有乘客提供饮用水。

This water carafe is identified with third class due to its limited decoration. Drinking water for all passengers was provided by carafes located in public and dining areas.

瓶和罐
Jars and Jugs

啤酒瓶
来源： 英国
年代： 爱德华时期，1912 年
尺寸： ① 22.38 厘米 x 7.30 厘米
② 22.70 厘米 x 7.46 厘米

Beer Bottles
Origin: United Kingdom
Period: Edwardian Period, 1912
Size: ① 22.38 cm x 7.30 cm
② 22.70 cm x 7.46 cm

泰坦尼克号前往美国时携带了两万多瓶啤酒和麦酒。每杯酒售价 11 美分。

Titanic carried over 20,000 bottles of beer and ale on her voyage to the United States, which sold for 11 cents per glass.

①

②

133

酒 瓶

来源： 英国
年代： 爱德华时期，1912 年
尺寸： ① 32.54 厘米 x 8.09 厘米
② 27.94 厘米 x 7.62 厘米

Liqueur Bottles

Origin: United Kingdom
Period: Edwardian Period, 1912
Size: ① 32.54 cm x 8.09 cm
② 27.94 cm x 7.62 cm

泰坦尼克号携带了 850 瓶白酒作为其首航规定的一部分。鼓脖子形状的棕色瓶中装的可能是威士忌。透明的瓶子虽没有标签，但它的形状与装薄荷甜酒的瓶子一样。每个瓶里面都有瓶塞。

Titanic stocked 850 bottles of liquor as a part of its provisions for the maiden voyage. The brown bottle has a swell neck shape and probably held whiskey. Although the clear bottle has no label, its shape is the same as that of a mint liqueur bottle. The corks for each bottle are inside.

①

②

酒瓶

来源： 英国
年代： 爱德华时期，1912 年
尺寸： ① 30.79 厘米 x 7.46 厘米
② 32.70 厘米 x 8.73 厘米
③ 32.70 厘米 x 8.7 厘米

Wine Bottles

Origin: United Kingdom
Period: Edwardian Period, 1912
Size: ① 30.79 cm x 7.46 cm
② 32.70 cm x 8.73cm
③ 32.70 cm x 8.7 cm

①

②

③

葡萄酒和葡萄汽酒在爱德华时期非常流行。泰坦尼克号携带的酒足以满足乘客需求。这些瓶子的软木塞在泰坦尼克号沉没海底时，被强大的水压推到瓶子里。

Wines and sparkling wines were very popular in the Edwardian Period. *Titanic* carried a significant amount of wine to meet passenger needs.The corks of these bottles were pushed in by the incredible water pressure at the ocean floor where *Titanic* came to rest.

135

罐和瓶

来源： 英国
年代： 爱德华时期，1912 年
尺寸： ① 26.67 厘米 x 8.57 厘米
② 24.13 厘米 x 10.795 厘米
③ 25.4 厘米 x 8.57 厘米
④ 13.17 厘米 x 5.39 厘米
⑤ 26.03 厘米 x 8.89 厘米

Cans and Bottles

Origin: United Kingdom
Period: Edwardian Period, 1912
Size: ① 26.67 cm x 8.57 cm
② 24.13 cm x 10.795 cm
③ 25.4 cm x 8.57 cm
④ 13.17 cm x 5.39 cm
⑤ 26.03 cm x 8.89 cm

①

②

④

⑤

③

泰坦尼克号必须携带足够的物品以供所有乘客和工作人员使用。陶器和盐釉罐很可能是用来盛放各种油的。有软木塞的玻璃瓶上印有"MOUTARDE DIAPHANE LOUIT FRERES & CO",表明芥末调料产自法国。

Titanic had to carry enough provisions to serve all passengers and crew for the entire voyage. The earthenware and salt glazed jars were probably for various oils. The glass jar with the cork is stamped "MOUTARDE DIAPHANE LOUIT FRERES & Co," indicating a mustard condiment made in France.

137

冰山和救援

1912年4月14日，泰坦尼克号马可尼无线通信员收到至少5封来自北大西洋轮船的电报，通知他们该区域有异常巨大的冰山。所有电报都交到了船长手上。晚上10点55分加利福尼亚的通信员通知泰坦尼克号：因为被冰山包围，加利福尼亚号已经停止前进。不幸的是，泰坦尼克号的无线通信员因忙于发送个人信息，没有时间对这条信息做出反应。泰坦尼克号于晚上11点40分撞上冰山，到4月15日凌晨12点05分时确定船将沉没，并下达了准备救生艇的命令。史密斯船长命令无线通信员持续发送求救信号。然而只有三艘船做出了回应，其中卡帕西亚最近，距离为93千米。

当船下沉时，报务员多次发出求救信息，传达了遇难所在的海域地点和危险状况。只有一艘船足够近，回应了呼救电讯。尽管该船需要行驶4个小时才能赶到现场，而且行驶前方还有冰山，但还是加速驶向泰坦尼克号。这艘船名为卡帕西亚号（Carpathia），船长亚瑟·罗斯特（Arthur Rostron)收到求救呼叫后，命令船全速前进，以最快的速度赶往营救地点拯救伤员。当卡帕西亚号到达泰坦尼克号的出事海域时，只有20只救生艇和705名乘客和船员飘浮在冰冷的海水中。

ICEBERG AND RESCUE

Throughout the day of April 14, 1912, *Titanic's* Marconi wireless operators received at least five telegrams from ships in the North Atlantic that there was heavy ice in the area, more than was usual for the time of year. All reports were sent to the Captain. At 10:55 pm, the Californian's wireless operator notified *Titanic* that they were stopped and surrounded by ice. Sadly, *Titanic's* wireless operators were so busy sending personal messages that they did not have time to react to the news. *Titanic* struck the iceberg at 11:40 pm and by 12:05 on April 15 knew that the Ship would sink and ordered the lifeboats readied. Captain Smith then ordered the wireless operators to send distress signals continuously. Only three ships responded to the distress call and Carpathia was the closest—93 km away.

While *Titanic* was sinking, its operator telegraph sent distress messages repeatedly, indicating their location and condition. Only one boat was close enough to answer the call. Although four hours away, with a field of icebergs ahead, Carpathia began to accelerate towards *Titanic*. When he received the call, Captain Arthur Rostron sailed into treacherous waters at full speed in order to reach the Ship and rescue the wounded. When Carpathia reached *Titanic*, all that remained of the Ship were twenty lifeboats with 705 passengers and crew, scattered across the sea ice.

电报机

来源： 英国
年代： 爱德华时期，1912 年
尺寸： 高 72.4 厘米；直径 38.1 厘米
44 厘米 x 58 厘米 x 58 厘米

Emergency Engine Room Telegraph

Origin: United Kingdom
Period: Edwardian Period, 1912
Size: h. 72.4 cm; diam. 38.1 cm
44 cm x 58 cm x 58 cm

桥台电报机通过舰上指令键标有如"停"或"全速前进"的指示板和机房来进行沟通。这个设备会及时将船长的指令准确地传送到机电房。

此电报机主要是在主设备出故障的情况下备用。在船撞上冰山的那一晚，据说泰坦尼克号甲板上的人员同时使用主设备和紧急电报机传送"全速后退"的指令，提示工程师遇到了紧急情况。

The Bridge telegraph communicated with the Engine Room via a faceplate labeled with written Ship's instructions, like "Stop" or "Full Ahead." The device instantaneously sent the captain's messages to an identically configured faceplate in the Engine Room.

The primary purpose of this telegraph was to act as a backup in case of a cable failure of the main units. However, on the night of the collision, *Titanic's* deck officers reportedly threw both the main and the emergency telegraphs to "Full Astern" to show the engineers that they encountered an emergency.

方向盘支架

来源： 英国
年代： 爱德华时期，1912 年
尺寸： 88.26 厘米 x 37.15 厘米

Steering Wheel Stand

Origin: United Kingdom
Period: Edwardian Period, 1912
Size: 88.26 cm x 37.15 cm

这个方向盘支架位于船长室下面的导航室。支架上面是柚木方向盘，副手跟随史密斯(Smith) 船长的指令操纵方向盘。1912 年 4 月 14 日，副手罗伯特·亨彻斯（Robert Hichen）一直驾驶着泰坦尼克号平稳前行。

This steering wheel stand is from the Navigator's Bridge, located directly behind the Captain's Bridge.The stand supported a teak steering wheel which allowed the quartermasters to follow Captain Smith's directed course.Quartermaster Robert Hichens held *Titanic* steady through the night watch on April 14, 1912.

PRESS PLUNGER
TO CALL
DISTANT STATION
PATENT NAVYPHONE
ALFRED GRAHAM & Co LONDON

黄铜挂式电话

来源： 英国
年代： 爱德华时期，1912 年
尺寸： 50.16 厘米 x 16.51 厘米 x 20.35 厘米

Bronze Wall Telephone

Origin: United Kingdom
Period: 1912, Edwardian Period
Size: 50.16 cm x 16.51 cm x 20.35 cm

电话用于泰坦尼克号上工作室之间的交流。该电话的工作原理很像一部对讲机：一部电话机通常只对一个遥控站进行通信，不需要交换台。研究认为，这部电话位于桅杆处，直接连线到指挥台。瞭望员弗雷德里克（Frederick Fleet）正是用这部电话机通知指挥室正前方有冰山。它有一个扩音话筒，接线盒在下方，左右分别有喇叭状听筒用线挂在耳朵上，现只保存了右侧听筒。

Telephones were used for contecting between working compartments on *Titanic*. The phone works much like an intercom: a single phone generally communicates with only one remote station, eliminating the need for a switchboard. It is believed that this telephone was located in the crow's nest with a direct line to the Bridge. Lookout Frederick Fleet used this phone to advise the Bridge there was an iceberg straight ahead. It has a megaphone-like mouthpiece and a junction box below. On the right and left were trumpet-shaped ear pieces with hinges for placement over the ears but only the right side survived.

泰坦尼克号的计时钟

来源： 英国
年代： 爱德华时期，1912 年
尺寸： 7.63 厘米 x 12.7 厘米

Titanic's Chronometer

Origin: United Kingdom
Period: Edwardian Period, 1912
Size: 7.63 cm x 12.7 cm

21 点，史密斯（Smith）船长在航行图上记录了轮船在 19 点 30 分时的位置，这个位置是之前四副鲍豪尔（Boxhall）绘制的。不久后，船长就回房间休息了。计时钟是轮船上指挥室用于导航的高度精确的时钟。通过计时钟与本地时间比较，船上人员能够确定该船从伦敦出发以来向东或向西走了多远。

泰坦尼克号上有两个这样的计时钟，都是由 J.W 雷公司制造的，两个都安装在海图室的特制盒子里，而海图室位于装有主舵盘的指挥室后面。只有一个计时钟被打捞上来。在船上指挥台浸入水中时，指针冻结了，这表明当时泰坦尼克号正开往美国，船员已经将该钟设置为华盛顿国家观测台时间。

At 21:00 Captain Smith recorded the 19:30 Ship's position on the navigational chart, which had earlier been plotted by Fourth Officer Boxhall. Soon after, the Captain retired to his quarters. Chronometers were highly accurate clocks kept on the bridge of steamships to aid in navigation. By comparing the vessel's local time with the chronometer, officers on board could determine how far east or west the Ship had traveled from London.

Titanic carried two of these chronometers; both made by J. W. Ray and both mounted in a special case in the chart room, right behind the main steering wheel on the bridge. Only one has been recovered. The hands were frozen at the time the Ship's Bridge submerged, indicating that as *Titanic* approached the United States, its officers had already set this clock to match the one at Washington DC's National Observatory.

金属发簪

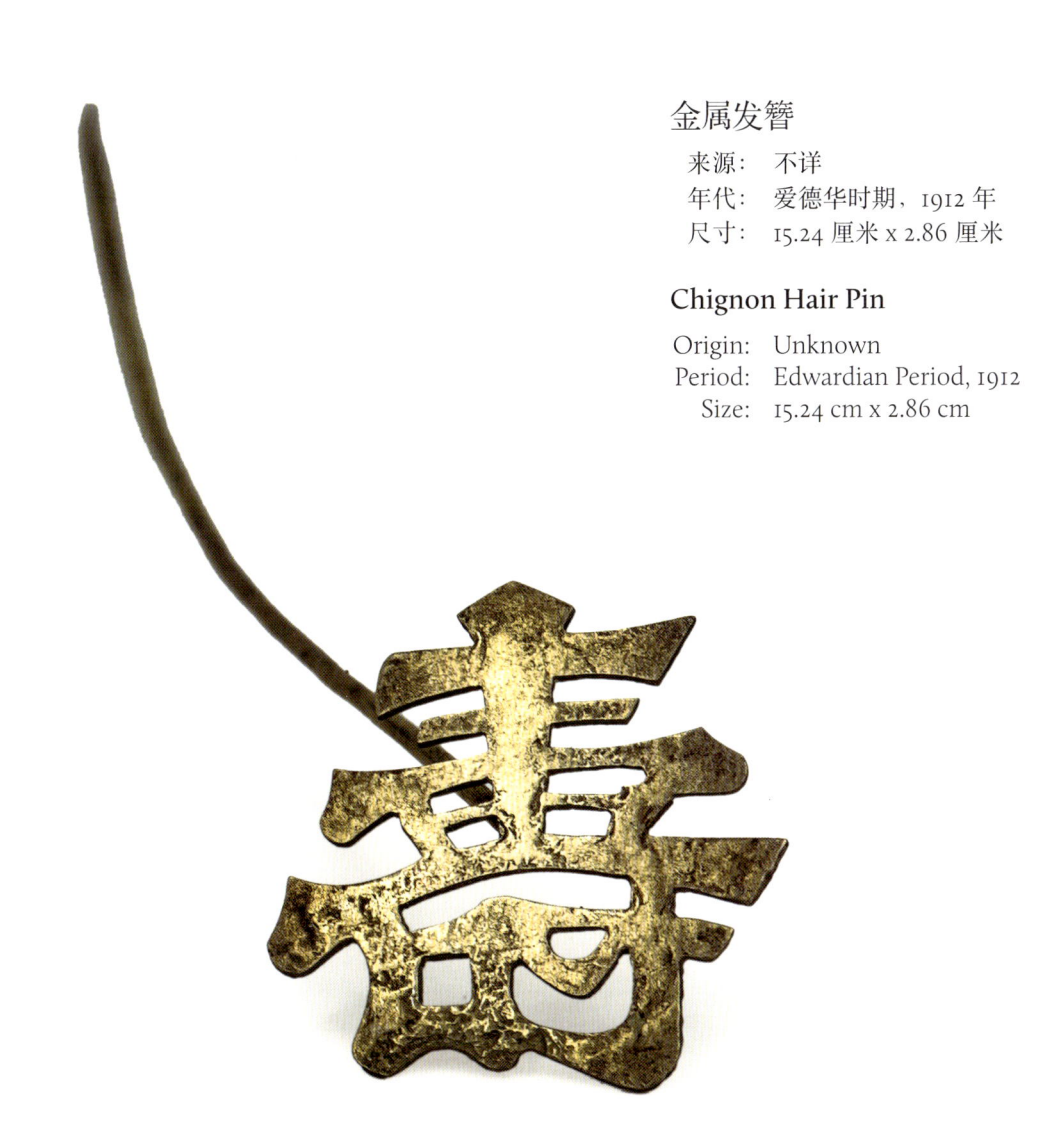

来源： 不详
年代： 爱德华时期，1912 年
尺寸： 15.24 厘米 x 2.86 厘米

Chignon Hair Pin

Origin: Unknown
Period: Edwardian Period, 1912
Size: 15.24 cm x 2.86 cm

一位乘客也许作为纪念品购买了这个发簪。装饰的中文"寿"字是长寿的意思。

A passenger may have purchased this hair pin as a souvenir. The decorative Chinese ideogram stands for "long life."

"艾米" 手链
来源： 英国
年代： 爱德华时期，1912 年
尺寸： 17.14 厘米 x 0.43 厘米

"Amy" Bracelet
Origin:　United Kingdom
Period:　Edwardian Period, 1912
　Size:　17.14 cm x 0.43 cm

这条漂亮的手链是由纯银和玫瑰金镶嵌钻石，钻石上刻有艾米 (Amy) 字样。链子由曲环和保险环组成。

This beautiful bracelet is constructed of pure silver over rose gold with diamonds. The name "Amy" is written in script and set with diamonds. It has a curb link chain with a safety chain.

146

皮制眼镜盒

来源： 法国
年代： 爱德华时期，1912 年
尺寸： 12.7 厘米 x 5.72 厘米

Leather glasses Case

Origin: France
Period: Edwardian Period, 1912
Size: 12.7 cm x 5.72 cm

夹鼻眼镜是在这个皮制的眼镜盒里找到的。其上的铭文显示，眼镜是在法国巴黎上昂格尔州里沃利街制作。

The pince nez glasses were recovered in this leather finish case. Its inscription states it was made at Unger Opticians on Rue de Rivoli, Paris, France.

眼 镜

来源： 法国
年代： 爱德华时期，1912 年
尺寸： 10.32 厘米 x 1.27 厘米 x 3.50 厘米

Pair of Spectacles

Origin: France
Period: Edwardian Period, 1912
Size: 10.32 cm x 1.27 cm x 3.50 cm

这种风格的金丝眼镜被称为"夹鼻眼镜"，在十九世纪非常流行。两个镜片由弯曲的、比较灵活的 C 形金属桥架连接。金属桥在没有眼镜腿的情况下也可以将眼镜架在鼻子上。

This style of gold spectacles, called "pince-nez," were popular in the nineteenth century. They are in the C-bridge style, which had a C-shaped bridge of curved, flexible metal. This bridge provided the tension needed for the spectacles to stay in place without the temples around the ears.

木制衣夹

来源： 英国
年代： 爱德华时期，1912 年
尺寸： 不同尺寸

Wooden Clothes Pins

Origin: United Kingdom
Period: Edwardian Period, 1912
Size: Various sizes

在一位可能要移民美国的乘客行李箱中发现了一些这样的衣夹。同时发现的还有磨石、测量棒、一包泻盐以及残缺不全的时间卡。只有木材部分幸存下来，金属弹簧在盐水中被腐蚀掉了。

These clothes pins were found in the luggage of passenger who migh have immigrated to the United States. At the same time, there are sharpening stone, measuring sticks, a package of Epsom Salts, and a fragmentary time card. Only the wood parts survived, the metal springs corroded in the salt water.

单簧管的两个部分

来源： 英国
年代： 爱德华时期，1912 年
尺寸： 34.29 厘米 x 6.98 厘米；34.29 厘米 x 5.08 厘米

Two Parts of a Clarionet

Origin:　United Kingdom
Period:　Edwardian Period, 1912
　Size:　34.29 cm x 6.98 cm; 34.29 cm x 5.08 cm

一百年前，木管乐器不像现在这样规范。键和手指垫的排列是逐步复杂化以适应演奏者的技能。这种乐器在当时被称为单簧管，其键盘系统适合高水平的业余演奏者。绿色的腐蚀物已经附着在部分部件上。

One hundred years ago, woodwind instruments were not standardized as today. The arrangement of keys and finger pads was graduated in complexity to match the skill of the player. This "clarionet" as the instrument was called at the time, has a key system consistent with the playing skills of an advanced amateur. The copper elements have green corrosion products attached.

149

双把花瓶

来源： 英国
年代： 爱德华时期、1912 年
尺寸： 18.41 厘米 x 10.79 厘米

Vase with Two Handles

Origin:　United Kingdom
Period:　Edwardian Period, 1912
Size:　18.41 cm x 10.79 cm

这个花瓶是属于泰坦尼克号上一名乘客的。它有一个漏斗口和两个 C 形把手，瓶身有鲜花和花环珠，瓶颈部和底座的琉璃从蓝色渐变为绿色、黄色。

This vase belonged to a passenger on *Titanic*. It has a funnel mouth and two C-scroll handles, while the body has flowers and bead garlands. The neck and base are accented with colored glaze changing from blue to green to yellow.

这个酒具有模糊的"自然主义"风格。陶瓷酒具由不规则的轮廓和浮雕枝叶组成。画面上身着多姿多彩古典服装的妇女举起酒杯向来宾敬酒,其手抱乐器,脚下匍匐着小天使。

This ceramic pitcher in a vaguely "naturalistic" style had a molded body with irregular contours and embossed foliage. The multicolored transfer depicts a woman in classical costume raising a glass of wine to toast an imaginary guest, while cradling a musical instrument by her side and a cherub at her feet.

酒具

来源: 英国
年代: 爱德华时期,1912 年
尺寸: 13.49 厘米 x 9.84 厘米

Wine Pitcher with Transfer Print

Origin: United Kingdom
Period: Edwardian Period, 1912
Size: 13.49 cm x 9.84 cm

鹅毛牙签

来源： 欧洲
年代： 爱德华时期，1912 年
尺寸： 长 8.25 厘米；直径 2.54 厘米

Bundle of Sharpened Goose Quills

Origin: Europe
Period: Edwardian Period, 1912
Size: l.8.25 cm; diam. 2.54 cm

鹅毛羽茎在历史上应用广泛。这些被削尖的鹅羽茎用作牙签，由棉线捆在一起存放。

Goose quills have been widely used in history. These quills were sharpened to be used as toothpicks. They are held in a bundle by cotton string.

人造象牙时钟房

来源： 法国
年代： 爱德华时期，1912 年
尺寸： 9.21 厘米 x 6.83 厘米 x 10.95 厘米

Synthetic Ivory Clock Housing

Origin: France
Period: Edwardian Period, 1912
Size: 9.21 cm x 6.83 cm x 10.95 cm

人造象牙时钟房由早期设计的类似象牙质地的塑料制成。这些塔状的房子被称为"马车钟"，是 1912 年旅游计时器的流行款式，上面刻有"法国御科特迪瓦"（Royal Ivoire France）。该时钟已经丢失了。

The synthetic ivory clock housing is made of early-designed ivory-like plastic. These tower-shaped cases were called "carriage clocks," were a popular style of traveling timepiece in 1912. This example is stamped "Royal Ivoire France." The clock is missing.

男性右脚鞋

来源： 欧洲
年代： 爱德华时期，1912 年
尺寸： 28.89 厘米 x 10.31 厘米 x 15.24 厘米

Man's Right Shoe

Origin: Europe
Period: Edwardian Period, 1912
Size: 28.89 cm x 10.31 cm x 15.24 cm

这只右脚男款皮鞋是对在泰坦尼克号上失去生命的人的凄美怀念。它是一只皮底的系带鞋。

A single man's right leather shoe is a poignant reminder of lives lost on *Titanic*. It is a lace-up shoe with a leather heel.

①

②

可折叠大礼帽和丝领结

来源： 英国
年代： 爱德华时期，1912 年
尺寸： ① 12.7 厘米 x 3.81 厘米 x 1.58 厘米
② 17.14 厘米 x 30.48 厘米

Collapsible Top Hat and Silk Bow Tie

Origin: United Kingdom
Period: Edwardian Period, 1912
Size: ① 12.7 cm x 3.81 cm x 1.58 cm
② 17.14 cm x 30.48 cm

礼帽在泰坦尼克号航行时代是常见的时尚配饰。礼帽通常由社会上层人士佩戴，除了追求时尚之外，也表明一个人的身份。丝绸领结在爱德华时代也很流行，是人们听歌剧或旅行时的常见装饰。这顶帽子是由著名的伦敦赫伯特·约翰逊帽子公司 (Herbert Johnson of London) 制作的。丝质领结适用于正式场合。

Top hats were still a common fashion accessory at the time of *Titanic's* sailing. Usually worn by the upper levels of society, the top hat in addition to being fashionable also indicated class. The silk collapsible version was popular in the Edwardian period for taking to the opera or on travels. This hat was made by the well-known hatter, Herbert Johnson of London. The silk bow tie would have completed the formal attire.

小狗

来源： 英国
年代： 爱德华时期，1912 年
尺寸： 6.03 厘米 x 2.38 厘米 x 5.4 厘米

Miniature Dog Figurine

Origin: United Kingdom
Period: Edwardian Period, 1912
Size: 6.03 cm x 2.38 cm x 5.4 cm

这个微型的小狗形状饰物属于泰坦尼克号上的一位乘客。

The miniature dog figurine displayed here belonged to one of *Titanic's* passengers.

青花瓷盘

来源： 英国
年代： 爱德华时期，1912 年
尺寸： 高 1.74 厘米；直径 14.44 厘米

Blue Emerald Plate

Origin: United Kingdom
Period: Edwardian Period, 1912
Size: h. 1.74 cm; diam. 14.44 cm

这个小碟子是乘客用的茶具，由英国当时的主要制造商亨利·阿尔科克 (Henry Alcock) 制作，图案名称"翡翠"是指碟子的风格，而不是指色彩。

This saucer belongs to a passenger's tea set. Made by Henry Alcock of England, a major manufacturer of the time, the pattern name "Emerald" refers to the style of the dish, not the color of the decoration.

海底和发现

皇家邮轮泰坦尼克号是在1912年4月15日凌晨2:20分，断裂为两部分沉没于北大西洋海平面以下3800米的海底，周围散落着很多私人物品和船体残骸。73年来，泰坦尼克号是孤独而失落的。自从1985年发现沉船后，皇家邮轮泰坦尼克号公司，先后进行了8次打捞，一共收集了5500多件实物，并加以记录和保存。

SEABED and DISCOVERY

The RMS *Titanic* sank at 2:20 a.m. on 15 April 1912. *Titanic* lies in two separate sections at 3,800 meters depth in the North Atlantic and is surrounded by a debris field with personal items and pieces of the actual Ship. For 73 years, *Titanic* was alone and lost. Since the wreck was discovered in 1985, RMS *Titanic*, Inc. has made eight expeditions to recover more than 5,500 objects, which were carefully cataloged and preserved.

汤 锅

来源： 法国
年代： 爱德华时期，1912 年
尺寸： 38.1 厘米 x 52.07 厘米 x 38.1 厘米

Stock Pot

Origin: France
Period: Edwardian Period, 1912
Size: 38.1 cm x 52.07 cm x 38.1 cm

深底酱料锅

来源： 法国
年代： 爱德华时期，1912 年
尺寸： 27.94 厘米 x 32.54 厘米

Deep Sauce Pan

Origin: France
Period: Edwardian Period, 1912
Size: 27.94 cm x 32.54 cm

泰坦尼克号船上的厨房占据了甲板的很大空间，在航行期间需要准备 6 万 2 千多份饭菜。这么庞大的食物量使得船上用的锅碗瓢盆的尺寸也格外大。

这些铜制和锡制的汤锅和平底锅由 E. Dehillerin 公司制造。该公司坐落在巴黎市中心，现在仍然营业，维持同样的公司名字，地址依然位于法国巴黎 E. Dehillerin，Rue Coquillière 18 号，邮编：75001。

The galleys onboard *Titanic* covered large amounts of deck space and prepared over 62,000 meals during the crossing. This vast amount of food dictated that even the pots and pans be of exceptional size.

Both this copper and tin stock pot and sauce pan were manufactured by E. Dehillerin in central Paris. The company is in business today under the same name and trading at the same address: E. Dehillerin, 18 Rue Coquillière, 75001 Paris, France.

双耳盘

来源: 法国
年代: 爱德华时期，1912 年
尺寸: 3.81 厘米 x 15.55 厘米

Au Gratin Dishes

Origin: France
Period: Edwardian Period, 1912
Size: 3.81 cm x 15.55 cm

数以百计的碟盘，保存完好，在海底被发现时像多米诺骨牌一样一字排开。它们完整地存放在橱柜里，船体下沉时被埋在沙子里。随着时间的推移，橱柜的木材腐烂了，留下整齐地叠放在一起的盘子。这些盘子是用特殊的防火泥土烧制而成，耐高温，既实用又好看。泰坦尼克号的大厨们用这些碟盘盛装食物并呈现给乘客。盘碟都刻有法国福厄西（Foëcy, France）的名称。

Hundreds of these perfectly preserved au gratin dishes were recovered from the seabed, where they were found lined up like dominoes. The cabinet in which they were stored remained intact and settled in the sand during the sinking. Over time the cabinet's wood rotted away, leaving the dishes stacked neatly together. Made from special fireproof clay that could withstand intense heat, these dishes were practical and attractive, allowing *Titanic's* cooks to use them for both the preparation and presentation of meals. The dishes are stamped with the name of Foëcy, France.

甲板长椅扶手
来源： 英国
年代： 爱德华时期，1912 年
尺寸： ① 73.66 厘米 x 59.69 厘米 x 5.08 厘米
② 84.77 厘米 x 59.05 厘米 x 16.51 厘米

Two Deck Bench Supports
Origin: United Kingdom
Period: Edwardian Period, 1912
Size: ① 73.66 cm x 59.69 cm x 5.08 cm
② 84.77 cm x 59.05 cm x 16.51 cm

①

②

安装在泰坦尼克号上层甲板上的甲板长椅可以让乘客全方位地观看大海。甲板长椅由右扶手、中心支架和左扶手三个金属支架组成，用木板条连接起来组成座位和靠背。用螺栓将甲板长椅固定在甲板上，以防止长椅在汹涌的海浪中从轮船上掉入海中。这里展示的是长椅的左右扶手。

Deck benches placed on *Titanic's* upper decks afforded passengers a panoramic view of the ocean below. The deck benches consisted of three metal supports - a right armrest, center support, and left armrest - linked by wooden slats creating the seat and back support. The deck benches were bolted to the deck to keep from rolling off the Ship in heavy seas. Shown here are the right and left armrest supports from one of these benches.

船员舱窗户

来源： 英国
年代： 爱德华时期，1912 年
尺寸： 114.3 厘米 x 58.42 厘米

Officer's Cabin Window in Two Parts

Origin: United Kingdom
Period: Edwardian Period, 1912
Size: 114.3 cm x 58.42 cm

窗户由坚固的铜合金部件和厚重的玻璃制成，安装在甲板左舷船舱船员室。窗户底部可以用铰链打开，而顶部有一个通风窗，在天气恶劣时能让空气流通。

The window are made of robust copper alloy parts and heavy glass, and are installed in Officer's Quarters on the Boat Deck. The bottom portion of the window could be hinged open, while the top section was a transom that allowed for ventilation in case of bad weather.

头等舱舷窗框

来源： 英国
年代： 爱德华时期，1912 年
尺寸： 69.85 厘米 x 54.61 厘米 x 12.7 厘米

First Class Porthole Frame

Origin: United Kingdom
Period: Edwardian Period, 1912
Size: 69.85 cm x 54.61 cm x 12.7 cm

这种类型的舷窗仅在价格比较高昂的头等舱和二等舱的餐厅里才能见到。窗的玻璃非常大，可让乘客看到大海。舷窗是可调的，以便让海上清新的空气进来。

This type of porthole is a pivot port that was found only in more expensive first-class cabins and in the Second Class Dining Saloon. The porthole is unusual in that it is both large enough to afford a view of the ocean and adjustable so that the glass can pivot to form a scoop and admit sea air into the room.

纪 念

　　泰坦尼克号沉没几天后，全世界都得知了这个悲惨的消息，1523人丧生，705人获救。全世界都在哀悼。为此，人们建立了基金会用来帮助那些需要资助的幸存者。各国政府自此海难后，制定了新的海事法律：确保船上提供足够的救生艇，以保证全体乘客和船员逃生；规定定期进行救生艇演习；要保证电报一天24小时处于通信状态；提供标准的遇险信号火箭的颜色。泰坦尼克号的事故，也促成了一个国际冰险巡逻队的建立，这确保自1914年以后其他船舶不再遭遇泰坦尼克号的厄运。

　　泰坦尼克号上船员和乘客的私人物品讲述着它们主人的故事。睹物思人，联想和感叹这些乘客的命运，产生一种挥之不去的情感共鸣，令人难忘！

MEMORY

A few days after the sinking of *Titanic*, the world learned the tragic news that 1,523 lives were lost and 705 rescued. The world mourned the loss, while funds were collected to help needy survivors. Governments were galvanized into action with new maritime laws: ensure that sufficient lifeboats for all on board were provided; conduct regular lifeboats exercises; maintain telegraph communication 24 hours a day, and provide standard distress rocket colors. *Titanic's* fate also contributed to the establishment of an international ice patrol, which has ensured that no other ship suffered *Titanic's* fate since 1914.

The artifacts that have been recovered and that can be directly linked to a particular passenger or crew member from *Titanic* are highlighted to continue the legacy of *Titanic* and all who sailed on her.

绿色玻璃墨水瓶

来源： 美国
年代： 爱德华时期，1912 年
尺寸： 长 6.98 厘米；直径 7.31 厘米

Green Glass Ink Bottle Belonging to Edgar Samuel Andrew

Origin:　United States
Period:　Edwardian Period, 1912
　Size:　l. 6.98 cm; diam. 7.31 cm

虽然钢笔在 1912 年已开始普遍使用，很多人仍然从这样的墨水瓶里蘸取墨水，用硬鹅毛笔写字。这个墨水瓶属于名为埃德加·塞缪尔·安德鲁 (Edgar Samuel Andrew) 的学生。

Although pens had come into common usage in 1912, many people still wrote with steel quill pens, which were dipped into inkwells like the one on display here. This ink bottle belonged to the student Edgar Samuel Andrew.

香水标签和香水瓶

来源： 英国
年代： 爱德华时期，1912 年
尺寸： ① 4.60 厘米 x 0.95 厘米　② 4.60 厘米 x 0.95 厘米
　　　③ 4.45 厘米 x 0.95 厘米　④ 4.60 厘米 x 0.95 厘米
　　　⑤ 2.54 厘米 x 1.90 厘米　⑥ 2.54 厘米 x 1.90 厘米
　　　⑦ 2.38 厘米 x 1.75 厘米

Perfume Labels and Vials Belonging to Adolphe Saalfeld

Origin:　United Kingdom
Period:　Edwardian Period, 1912
Size:　① 4.60 cm x 0.95 cm　② 4.60 cm x 0.95 cm　③ 4.45 cm x 0.95 cm
　　　④ 4.60 cm x 0.95 cm　⑤ 2.54 cm x 1.90 cm　⑥ 2.54 cm x 1.90 cm
　　　⑦ 2.38 cm x 1.75 cm

尽管在海底沉睡了近 90 年，这些小瓶在打捞检查被打开时，仍然散发出芳香。

每个玻璃小瓶的香味都写在小瓶的标签上。玻璃瓶被依次装在一个金属圆柱里，然后保存在一个小皮盒内。再把玫瑰、熏衣草、佛手柑和其他天然植物油掺入香水里。这里的手写标签为：山谷百合花香型花油、铃兰花香型花油和红百里香香精。

Despite spending nearly nine decades on the ocean floor, these vials still emitted the scent of the oils they contained when examined during recovery.

Each glass vial contained one scent, identified by a label attached to the vial. The glass was in turn encased in a metal cylinder which was then stored in a small leather portfolio. The natural oils of rose, lavender, bergamot, and other plants were to be blended into perfumes. The hand-written labels here are for Floral Otto of Lily of the Valley, Floral Otto W and Thyme Red.

洛森西因 (Rosenshine) 旅行日程表
来源： 日本
年代： 爱德华时期，1912 年
尺寸： ① 15.56 厘米 x 11.43 厘米
② 15.24 厘米 x 13.17 厘米

Rosenshine Partial Itinerary

Origin: Japan
Period: Edwardian Period, 1912
Size: ① 15.56 cm x 11.43 cm
② 15.24 cm x 13.17 cm

当泰坦尼克沉没时，乔治·洛森西因 (George Rosenshine) 和马贝尔·索恩 (Mabelle Thorne) 正在以索恩夫妇的名义环球旅行。这是日本横滨的 Thos. Cook & Son 旅游公司为他们制定的"日本中东之旅"旅行日程表，详细介绍了 1911 年 11 月从香港到新加坡的行程，包括访问上海。

George Rosenshine and Mabelle Thorne were traveling around the world in the name of Mr. and Mrs. Thorne, when *Titanic* sank. These are two pages of a proposed travel itinerary for a "Japan to the Middle East" tour, prepared by Thos. Cook & Son, Yokohama, Japan, detailing the Hong Kong to Singapore leg, scheduled for November 1911. The tour also included a visit to Shanghai.

袜子

来源： 欧洲
年代： 爱德华时期，1912 年
尺寸： 37.78 厘米 x 25.7117 厘米

Pair of Socks

Origin: Europe
Period: Edwardian Period, 1912
Size: 37.78 cm x 25.7117 cm

这双米色丝袜从海底打捞上来，发现于弗兰兹·帕尔鲍姆 (Franz Pulbaum) 的手提箱里。这双丝袜从来没有被穿过，因为袜子的脚趾是缝合在一起的。这双丝袜很有可能是帕尔鲍姆在访问法国期间购买的。

This pair of beige silk socks was recovered in a Franz Pulbaum's suitcase. They were never worn as they are stitched together at the toe. It is most likely that they were purchased during Pulbaum's visit to France.

袖口带

来源： 欧洲
年代： 爱德华时期，1912 年
尺寸： 11.11 厘米 x 2.22 厘米

Pair of Sleeve Garters

Origin: Europe
Period: Edwardian Period, 1912
Size: 11.11 cm x 2.22 cm

在爱德华时代，男人成衣上有一条长袖口带。这种弹性带子是用来缩短袖子的，也有助于保持袖口清洁。

In the Edwardian period, men's ready-made shirts had a single long length. Elastic sleeve garters were used to shorten the sleeves and helped keep the cuffs clean.

巴黎纪念明信片

来源： 欧洲
年代： 爱德华时期，1912 年
尺寸： 13.97 厘米 x 8.89 厘米

Paris Souvenir Postcard

Origin: Europe
Period: Edwardian Period, 1912
Size: 13.97 cm x 8.89 cm

帕尔鲍姆 (Pulbaum) 访问巴黎时收集了纪念明信片。明信片中展示的是位于巴黎圣日耳曼德佩区的圣克洛蒂尔德教堂 (Saint-Germain-des-Prés)。它以宏伟的双尖塔而闻名，在背景中可以看到双尖塔。

Pulbaum collected souvenir postcards during he visit to Paris. This one shows the Basilica of Saint Clotilde in Paris, in the area of Saint-Germain-des-Prés. It is well known for its imposing twin spires, it can be seen in the background of the panoramic view.

《标准版家庭和学校用词典》

来源： 欧洲
年代： 爱德华时期、1912 年
尺寸： 21.59 厘米 x 16.51 厘米 x 5.08 厘米

"Standard Home and School Dictionary"

Origin:　Europe
Period:　Edwardian Period, 1912
　Size:　21.59 cm x 16.51 cm x 5.08 cm

作为来自德国的移民，帕尔鲍姆 (Pulbaum) 随身携带着一本图文并茂的英语词典。这本词典有一个带有金色字母的软皮封面。

As an immigrant from Germany, Pulbaum kept an illustrated English language dictionary with him. This dictionary has a soft leather cover with gold letter.

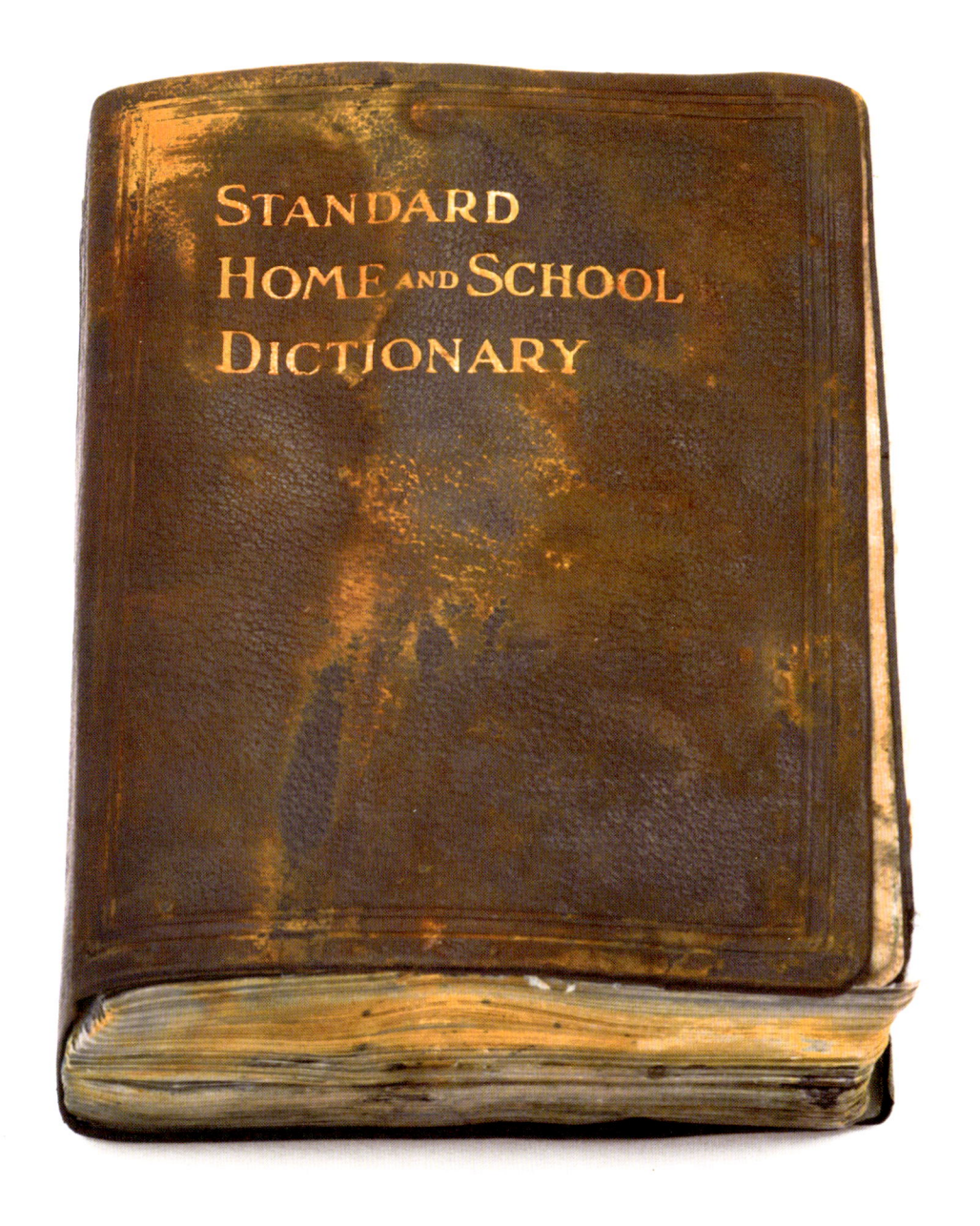

工具和护套

来源： 美国
年代： 爱德华时期，1910 年
尺寸： ① 9.20 厘米 x 3.02 厘米
② 16.19 厘米 x 0.63 厘米
③ 8.25 厘米 x 2.22 厘米

Tools and Sheath

Origin: United States
Period: Edwardian Period, 1910
Size: ① 9.20 cm x 3.02 cm
② 16.19 cm x 0.63 cm
③ 8.25 cm x 2.22 cm

这里展示的工具发现于霍华德·欧文（Howard Irwin）的行李箱里。霍华德·欧文是一个皮匠，他的行李箱里装满了工作用的工具以及明信片和乐器。皮护套里装有其中一个工具的手柄，发现时工具的金属部分已被海水腐蚀了。

The tools shown here were recovered from Howard Irwin's trunk, which was filled with tools for his work as a leather trimmer, as well as postcards and musical instruments. The leather sheath held one of the handles when recovered although all metal elements had corroded in the salt water.

霍华德·A. 欧文
(Howard A. Irwin) 来访卡片

来源： 美国
年代： 爱德华时期，1910 年
尺寸： 7.62 厘米 x 3.81 79 厘米

Calling Card of Howard A. Irwin

Origin: United States
Period: Edwardian Period, 1910
Size: 7.62 cm x 3.81 79 cm

类似于今天的名片，维多利亚时代成年人用来访卡保持中上层阶级社交与商业的联系。"来访卡"，是指当女主人不在家时，访客把卡留给女佣或门卫然后离开，以表明访客的身份。此卡上有霍华德 A. 欧文（Howard A. Irwin）的名字，他的家乡是纽约州 Buffalo 市，来访卡上的英文字母拼写错为"Baffalo"。

It's similar to today's postcard, the Victorian calling card was used by adults to maintain social and commercial links between upper and middle classes. "Calling card" refers to the custom of leaving the card with the maid or doorman to indicate who had "called" while the lady of the house was out. On this card with Howard A. Irwin's name, his home city of Buffalo, NY, is misspelled as "Baffalo."

①

明信片

来源： 美国
年代： 爱德华时期，1910 年
尺寸： ① 13.97 厘米 x 8.89 厘米　② 13.97 厘米 x 8.89 厘米

Postcards

Origin:　United States
Period:　Edwardian Period, 1910
　Size:　① 13.97 cm x 8.89 cm　② 13.97 cm x 8.89 cm

明信片是 19 世纪末期流行起来的人们之间的沟通交流方式。尽管大多数明信片都是著名的风景名胜，但也有一些社会评论如同这里所展示的这张明信片，以漂亮、浪漫的内容表达细腻的感情。第二张明信片描绘了加州长滩码头和长滩码头的阳光馆。这张里德尔明信片由乔治 O·雷斯塔尔（George O. Restall）出版，该公司专门出版绘制加州风景点的半色调版画。

Postcards were a popular form of communication starting in the last quarter of the 19th century. While many were souvenirs of famous places, some had social commentary and could be saucy or romantic to express delicate sentiments, such as the one here.The second postcard depicts Long Beach Pier and Sun Pavilion at Long Beach, California. It is a

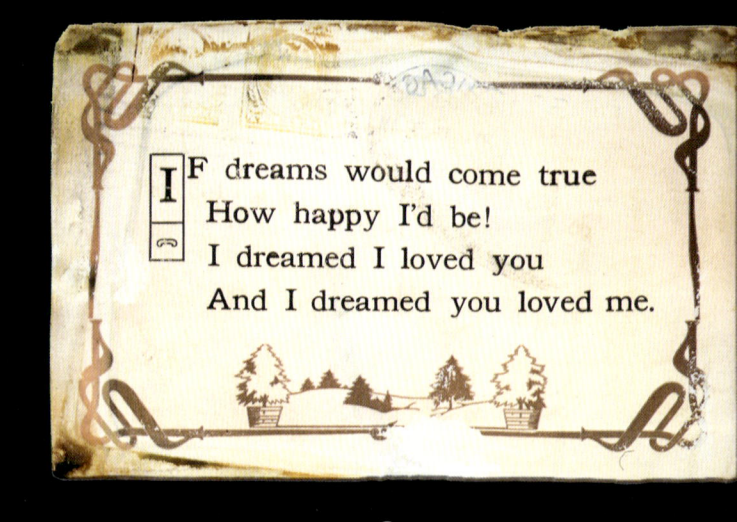

②

丝绸领带和男士衬衫衣领

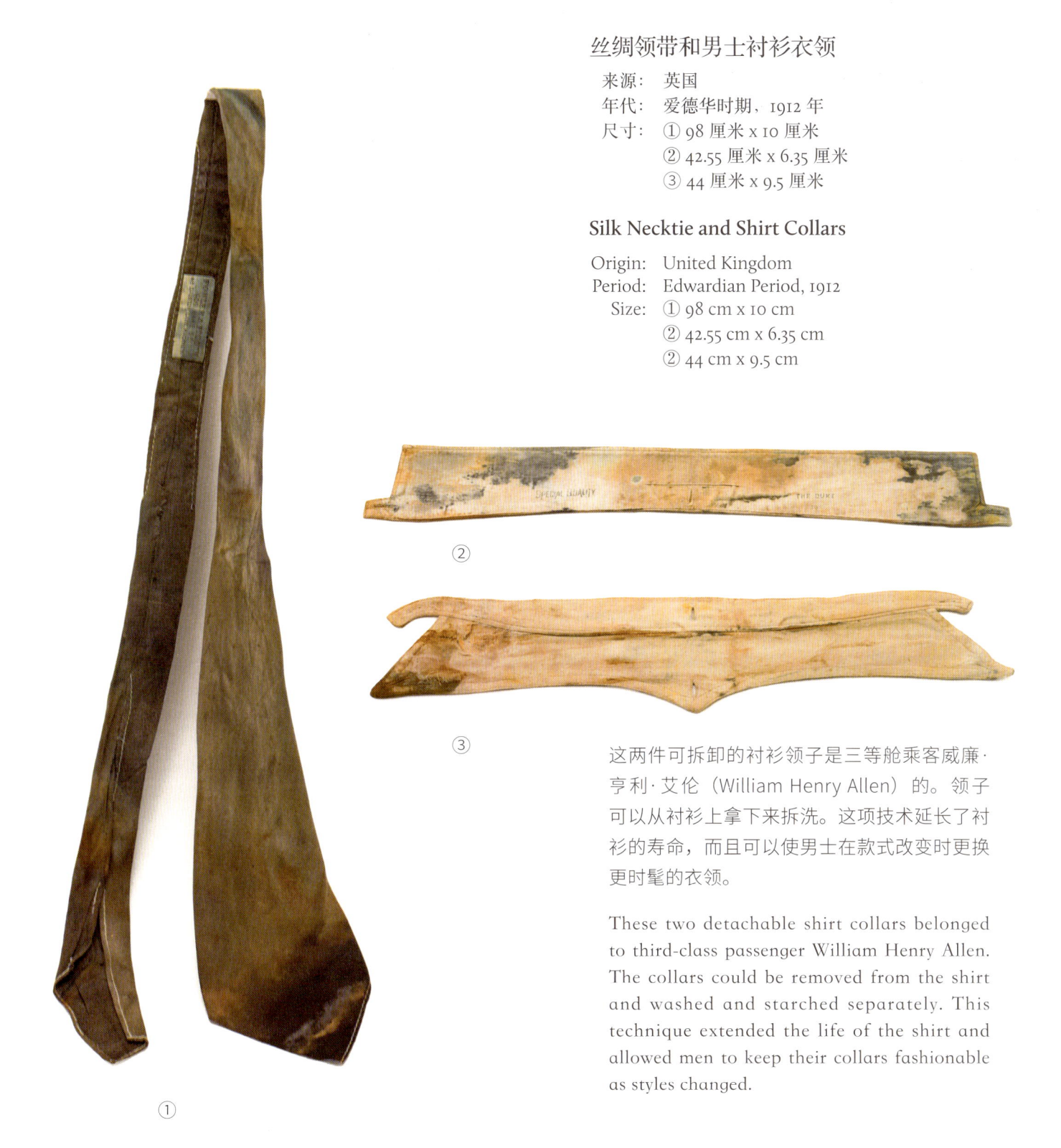

来源： 英国
年代： 爱德华时期，1912 年
尺寸： ① 98 厘米 x 10 厘米
② 42.55 厘米 x 6.35 厘米
③ 44 厘米 x 9.5 厘米

Silk Necktie and Shirt Collars

Origin: United Kingdom
Period: Edwardian Period, 1912
Size: ① 98 cm x 10 cm
② 42.55 cm x 6.35 cm
② 44 cm x 9.5 cm

①

②

③

这两件可拆卸的衬衫领子是三等舱乘客威廉·亨利·艾伦（William Henry Allen）的。领子可以从衬衫上拿下来拆洗。这项技术延长了衬衫的寿命，而且可以使男士在款式改变时更换更时髦的衣领。

These two detachable shirt collars belonged to third-class passenger William Henry Allen. The collars could be removed from the shirt and washed and starched separately. This technique extended the life of the shirt and allowed men to keep their collars fashionable as styles changed.

在日常生活中，男士穿着得体需要搭配一些配饰。背带是裤子前后面都有的附属物，用于支撑裤子。领子和袖口均可拆卸和更换，以方便清洁和延长衬衫的寿命。威廉·艾伦 (William Allen) 的手提箱里的领带有很多款式，从基本的棉制品到丝绸均有，袖口也可用袖扣扣起来。

Dressing appropriately required a number of accessories to complete a man's day suit. Braces, or suspenders, supported the trousers with attachments at the back and front. Collars and cuffs were both detachable and replaceable to facilitate cleaning and to extend the life of the shirt. William Allen had a selection of collars in his suitcase from basic cotton to silk, as well as cuffs that would be held together by cufflinks.

折叠小刀，微型左轮手枪，放大镜

来源： 英国
年代： 爱德华时期，1912 年
尺寸： ① 8.25 厘米 x 3.492 厘米 x 0.63 厘米
② 8.25 厘米 x 3.81 厘米 x 1.58 厘米
③ 7.62 厘米 x 1.59 厘米 x 1.27 厘米

Folding Pocket Knife and Miniature Revolver

Origin: United Kingdom
Period: Edwardian Period, 1912
Size: ① 8.25 cm x 3.492 cm x 0.63 cm
② 8.25 cm x 3.81 cm x 1.58 cm
③ 7.62 cm x 1.59 cm x 1.27 cm

霍尔特 (E.Holt) 来访卡片
来源： 英国
年代： 爱德华时期，1912 年
尺寸： 7.62 厘米 x 3.81 厘米

Calling Card of E. Holt
Origin:　United Kingdom
Period:　Edwardian Period, 1912
Size:　7.62 cm x 3.81 cm

马里恩·米恩韦尔 (Marion Meanwell) 的鳄鱼袋是 2000 年打捞上来的，里面有许多个人档案和文件，以及反映她个人的生活轨迹的文物。此来访卡属于霍尔特（E.Holt)，据推测是马里恩·米恩韦尔的一位亲戚。地址是老滑铁卢（英国利物浦的一家酒店）。

Marion Meanwell's alligator bag was recovered in 2000. Inside were many personal documents and papers as well as relics of her life. This card belonged to E. Holt, who is believed to be one of her relatives. The address is The Old Waterloo, a hotel in Liverpool, England.

这些小饰品发现于威廉·亨利·艾伦（Willliam Henry Allen）的物品中。微型手枪可能是一件纪念品或表带饰品。木制小刀外壳有镶铜设计。对于一名机械师和机器制造商而言，放大镜可能被用作工具。

These small trinkets were found among the belongings of William Henry Allen. The miniature pistol was probably a keepsake charm or fob. The wood pocket knife casing has a copper inset design. As a mechanic and machine maker, the magnifying glass would have been considered a tool.

佩斯利 (Paisley) 印花领巾

来源： 英国
年代： 爱德华时期，1912 年
尺寸： 78 厘米 x 78 厘米

Paisley Cravat

Origin: United Kingdom
Period: Edwardian Period, 1912
 Size: 78 cm x 78 cm

这条领巾是从三等舱一位名叫威廉·亨利·艾伦 (William H. Allen) 的手提箱中发现的，与其他 70 多件个人物品放在一起。最近对其进行修复，再现了其漂亮的红、黑色彩和佩斯利商标。领巾上挂了一个洗衣标签"W. 阿伦"。

领带流行于 19 世纪末，许多爱德华时代的绅士们认为领巾是一个基本的时尚配件。领巾的宽度和风格多种多样，从基本窄条款到宽款，以及有印花图案的褶边领巾。

This cravat was recovered from inside third class passenger William H. Allen's suitcase along with more than seventy other personal items. Recent conservation efforts have revealed the cravat's beautiful red and black colors and paisley print. It has a stamped laundry mark: "W. Allen."

Though neckties began to increase in popularity late in the nineteenth century, many Edwardian-era gentlemen considered the cravat a basic fashion accessory. Cravats ranged in width and style, from the basic thin strip to broad, frilly cravats with decorative prints.

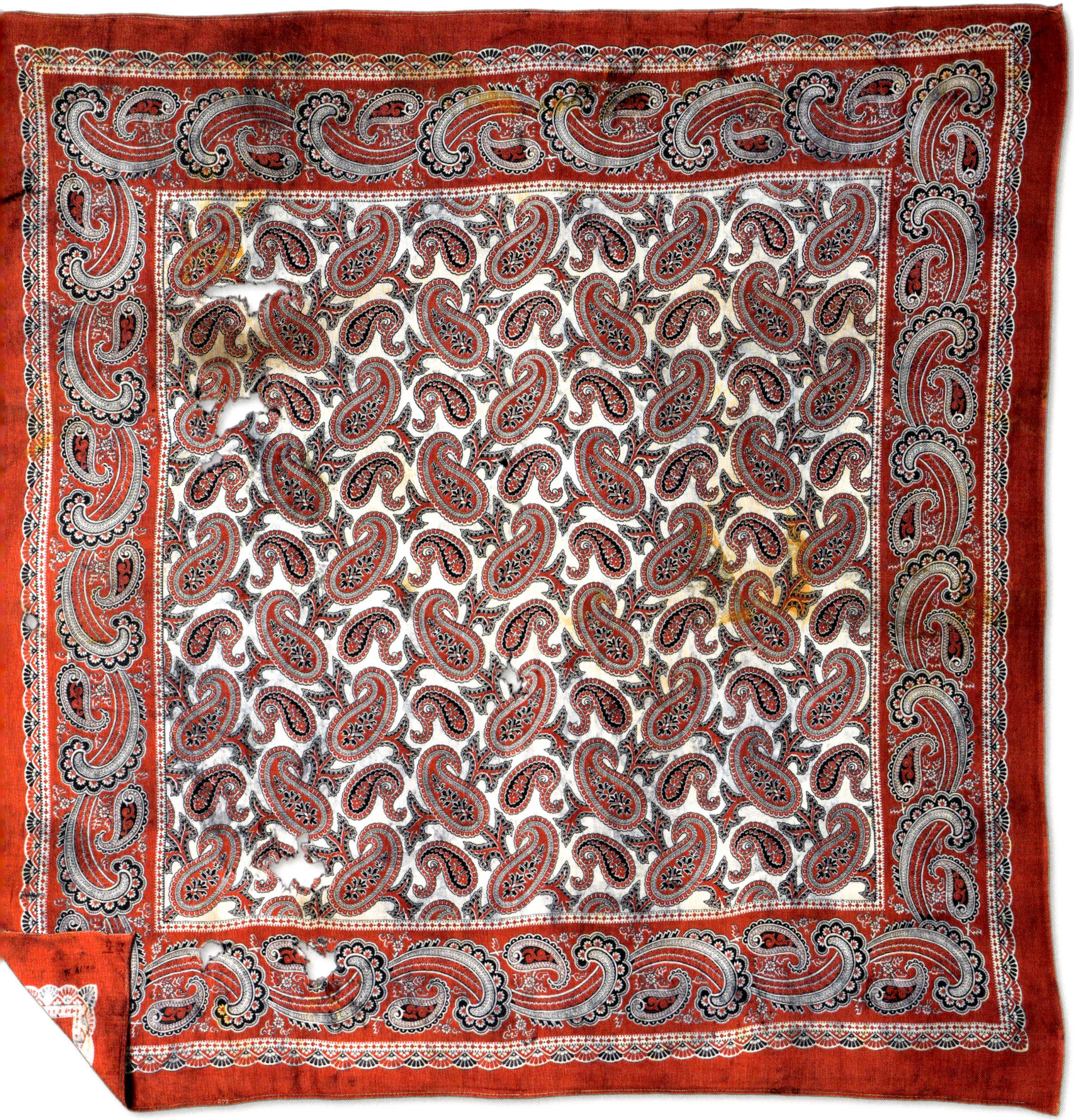

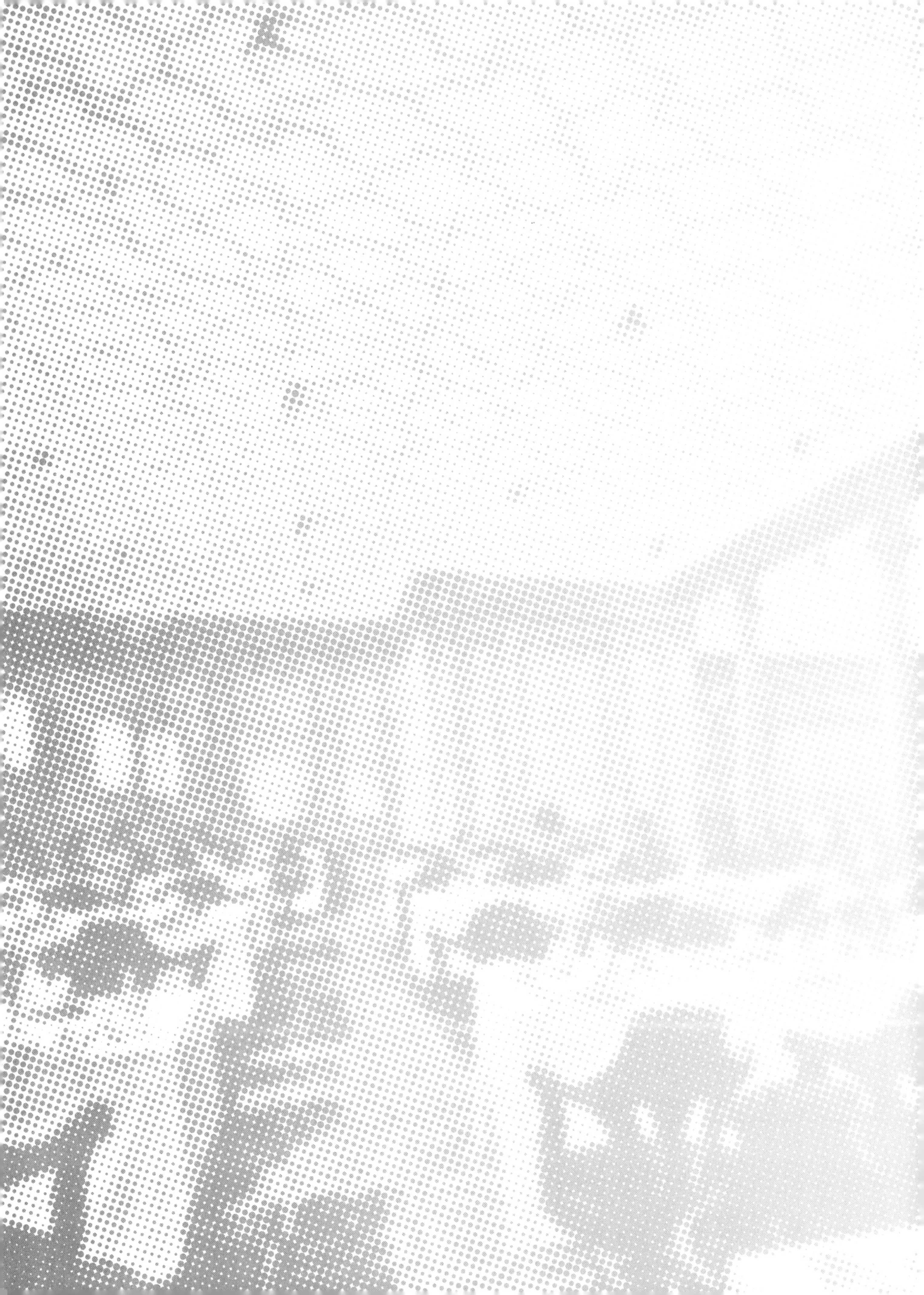

时间轴线

传奇诞生

船体部件

内部装潢

货物清单

船员信息

问题释疑

附录
APPENDIX

Titanic Timeline

Birth of *Titanic* Legend

Parts of the *Titanic*

Interior Decoration

Titanic Cargo Stats

Information on the Crew Members

TITANIC Frequently Asked Questions

时间轴线

1912年4月2日晚上8点，泰坦尼克号全体船员离开轮船的建造地贝尔法斯特，前往南安普顿参加试航。

1912年4月10日早上6点，太阳刚刚升起，第一批船员开始登上泰坦尼克号。除了史密斯Smith船长外，高级船员已经在船上住了一晚。史密斯Smith船长大约在当天早上7点30分到达。

1912年4月10日中午12点，泰坦尼克号开始首航，离开南开普敦，驶向法国瑟堡港和爱尔兰的昆斯顿（这是此船的官方启航日）。

1912年4月11日下午1点30分，泰坦尼克号最后一次起锚，离开了昆斯顿。

1912年4月14日晚上10点55分，加利福尼亚号完全被冰包围，在晚上停止前进，泰坦尼克号收到危险即将来临的警告。

1912年4月14日晚上11点40分，瞭望员弗雷德里克·弗利特Frederick Fleet看见冰山。

- 大副默多克下令"右满舵"，关闭引擎，转向减速，关闭防水门。
- 泰坦尼克号以20节（约26公里/时）的速度航行，稍微转向左方，避免了正面相撞。在水面以下，冰山撞击了船体。
- 五个，或许有六个密封舱涌进海水。

1912年4月15日凌晨12点15分，史密斯Smith船长评估损失

- 在估计船还剩2小时漂浮时间后，他命令电报员发出了求救信号："遇险，请速来救"。
- 他下令打开救生艇并撤离妇女和儿童。

1912年4月15日凌晨12点45分，第一艘救生艇离开泰坦尼克号，尽管可以装载65人，却只有19人登艇。

1912年4月15日凌晨2点05分，最后一艘救生艇放入水中，泰坦尼克号的船头开始下沉。大约1500人被困在了下沉中的巨轮上。

1912年4月15日凌晨2点20分，泰坦尼克号沉没。

报童手持沉船消息的报纸 /
Newsboy holding papers about the wre...

乘客家属焦急等待船上亲人的消息 /
Families of passengers waiting for wor...
on their loved ones onboard *Titanic*

遇难和幸存人数

总人数：2,228 人　幸存者总数：705 人　遇难者总数：1,523 人

	总数	幸存	遇难
一等舱	324	199	125
二等舱	284	116	168
三等舱	710	181	529
船员	910	209	701

TITANIC TIMELINE

April 2nd, 1912, 8:00 pm: The crew of *Titanic* participates in sea trials before leaving Belfast, where the Ship was built, for Southampton.

April 10th, 1912, 6:00 am: Just after sunrise the first members of the crew began to board *Titanic*. All of the officers except Captain Smith had already spent the night on board. Captain Smith arrived later that morning around 7:30.

April 10th, 1912, 12:00 pm: *Titanic* starts her maiden voyage, leaving Southampton and ventures to Cherbourg, France, and Queenstown, Ireland (this is the official sailing date for the Ship).

April 11th, 1912, 1:30 pm: *Titanic* raises anchor for the last time and leaves Queenstown.

April 14th, 1912, 10:55 pm: *Californian*, completely surrounded by ice, stops for the evening and warns the *Titanic* of the impending danger.

April 14th, 1912, 11:40 pm: Frederick Fleet sights an iceberg.

- First Officer Murdoch gives the "hard a-starboard" order while having the engines stopped and reversed; activates lever that closes watertight doors.
- The Ship, traveling at approximately 20 knots (26 mph), turned slightly to the left, avoiding a head-on collision. Below the water the iceberg punctures the hull.
- Five, possibly six of the *Titanic's* watertight compartments flood.

April 15th, 1912, 12:15 am: Captain Smith assesses the damage.

- He orders his telegraph operators to send the distress signal, "CQD," after estimating the Ship will remain afloat for two hours.
- He gives the order to uncover the lifeboats and evacuate the women and children.

April 15th, 1912, 12:45 am: First lifeboat leaves the Ship with only nineteen aboard, although it could carry sixty-five.

April 15th, 1912, 2:05 am: *Titanic's* bow begins sinking as the last of the lifeboats are lowered into the water. An estimated 1,500 people were left stranded on the sinking boat.

April 15th, 1912, 2:20 am: *Titanic* sinks.

Passenger and Crew Statistics

Total on board: 2,228   Total saved: 705   Total lost: 1,523

	Total	Saved	Lost
First Class	324	199	125
Second Class	284	116	168
Third Class	710	181	529
Crew	910	209	701

传奇诞生

二十世纪初，科技创造了包括汽车、飞机、电影院及电报等众多奇迹。在现代大型喷气式客机出现以前，跨洋运输采用的是远洋班轮，它们的速度比以往更快，体积更大，而且更豪华，可以适应当时的运输要求。

在1907年的一次夏季晚宴上，白星航运公司主席J. Bruce Ismay和哈兰德·沃尔夫造船厂所属的贝尔法斯特造船公司的合伙人Lord William J.Pirrie一起构思了一个计划，欲在前往北大西洋的客运旅游业中占据领先地位。他们计划建造有史以来最大和最豪华的三艘轮船。其中两艘轮船的建造工作即将开始。这两艘轮船的名称分别是奥林匹克号与泰坦尼克号。

泰坦尼克号及其姐妹船是在哈兰德·沃尔夫的绘图室设计的。在这个绘图室里，总经理Thomas Andrews, Jr.负责监督绘图员、描图员、制表人及蓝图绘制员团队，因为他们要为奥林匹克号、泰坦尼克号及不列颠号绘制数千张图纸。设计这些轮船时，Andrews指示他的部门在设计时要达到力与美的巧妙平衡。作为有史以来建造的最大轮船，泰坦尼克号必须设计得足够坚固，能够在北大西洋波涛汹涌的海面上轻松航行。同时，作为有史以来建造的最豪华轮船，泰坦尼克号则必须超越最富有的乘客们的预期。

哈兰德·沃尔夫造船厂用全世界最大的起重机架搭建泰坦尼克号。10000多人用近3年时间建造了轮船船体与内部结构。船体平地而起，首先是龙骨和底板，然后安装肋拱、内部主梁，最后安装外部钢板。

高架起重机将大型钢板放置到位，由300多万颗铆钉将这些钢板固定。哈兰德·沃尔夫造船厂主要采用了新的液压铆接方法，但对于机器难以企及的部分，仍然使用手工锤击的方法铆入。建造人员利用液压铆接机固定钢铆钉，并采用手工锤击的方式固定更具延展性的铁铆钉。这种材料上的差异可能会造成了牢固性的差异。

为了满足巨大的姐妹船奥林匹克号与泰坦尼克号的建造要求，需要对哈兰德·沃尔夫的贝尔法斯特造船厂进行一些改造。其中一项是，需要建造两个巨大的新滑道，新滑道的施工于1907年开始。船厂拆散了三个小滑道，并将其合并为两个大滑道——2号及3号滑道，这为同时建造两艘轮船提供了足够的空间。新滑道的地面还覆盖了厚达1.35米的混凝土。1908年，一个必备的巨大起重机架安装完成。整体结构高达70米，重约1200000千克，同时配备了四个大型电动升降机和一个起重机系统。

哈兰德·沃尔夫造船厂从德国购入了200000千克的浮吊，能够将发动机、锅炉与烟囱装备起吊到奥林匹克号及泰坦尼克号上。维多利亚码头前两艘轮船下水沿线的沟渠也需要改造。该沟渠原本设计成4.5米深，以应对春天涨潮，但为满足建

J. Bruce Ismay

哈兰德·沃尔夫绘图室在绘制泰坦尼克号图纸 / Harland & Wolff Drawing Office where plans for *Titanic* were prepared

184

Lord William J. Pirrie

造两艘巨大轮船的需要，深挖沟渠至15米，而且码头结构也需要加固。

1911年5月31日，10万多人聚集在一起，见证泰坦尼克号的下水盛况。中午12:30，红色火箭疾驰升空，固定泰坦尼克号在船坞上的液压触发器被松开了。在轮船汽笛长鸣的欢庆声和拉根河两岸观众的一片惊叹声中，泰坦尼克号在早已涂满22000千克牛脂和肥皂的滑道中，以优雅的姿态轻松滑入了拉根河中。虽然已经下水，但泰坦尼克号离完工还相差甚远：内部装修尚未完成，而且轮船的发动机、锅炉、螺旋桨及四个烟囱尚未安装。泰坦尼克号距离整体完工还需要10个月工期。

下水后，泰坦尼克号依然是一个空壳。在未来的十个月里，超过3000名木匠、工程师、电工、水管工、油漆工、熟练技工，包括内部设计师的各类专业技工将辛勤工作，为泰坦尼克号装配最新的航海技术、最豪华的设施和家具。轮船的烟囱、机械装置及所有精密的设备也将安装到位。

在码头舾装期间，泰坦尼克号业主将轮船的32个救生艇减少到16个（这是英国法律要求的数量）。虽然也额外增加了4个可折叠的帆布救生艇，但白星航运公司的这个决定意味着仅为船上三分之一的人提供了逃生设施。

泰坦尼克号于1912年4月2日傍晚驶离了贝尔法斯特港。此前，轮船进行了包括在高速行驶时执行反转发动机命令试航测试。晚上8点，泰坦尼克号驶离了它的诞生地——大的工业城市贝尔法斯特港，驶向南安普敦。轮船在拉根河上航行，进入爱尔兰海域时，发动机发出巨大的隆隆声。整个夜晚，巨轮保持18节的稳定航速，而船上的马可尼无线电发报机则在不停地发出欢庆的捷报。泰坦尼克号传出的有些信息可传到4,800千米以外。

1912年4月10日星期三，英国南安普敦的码头上热闹非凡。清晨，泰坦尼克号全体船员开始登船，前往各自的工作岗位。很多二等舱及三等舱的乘客乘坐上午9点半从伦敦发出的火车抵达南安普敦，而大多数头等舱乘客则从容地乘坐上午11点半的火车抵达南安普敦，轮船管弦乐队演奏欢庆的音乐欢迎他们登船。上午时分，泰坦尼克号开始了它的处女航，穿过北大西洋，开往纽约。

泰坦尼克号和奥林匹克号在贝尔法斯特港的哈兰德-沃尔夫造船厂进行建造 /
Titanic and *Olympic* under construction in the Harland & Wolff shipyard in Belfast

BIRTH OF TITANIC LEGEND

At the beginning of the twentieth century, technology had brought about such wonders as the automobile, airplane, skyscraper, cinema, and telegraph. The world was on the move and transatlantic transport of passengers, cargo, and mail was brisk and competitive. Ocean liners, the predecessors of our modern day jumbo jets, became ever faster, larger, and more luxurious to accommodate this traffic.

At a dinner party in the summer of 1907, J. Bruce Ismay, chairman of the White Star Line, and Lord William J. Pirrie, a partner in the Belfast ship building firm of Harland & Wolff, conceived a plan to dominate passenger travel on the North Atlantic. They planned to construct three ships and start work immediately, desiring them to be the largest and most luxurious ever built. They would be called Olympic and Titanic.

Titanic and her sister ships were designed in the Drawing Office at Harland & Wolff. Here, Managing Director Thomas Andrews, Jr. supervised an army of drafters, tracers, tabulators, and blueprint makers as they produced the thousands of drawings that would become Olympic, Titanic, and Britannic. In designing these ships, Andrews directed his department to strike a delicate balance between strength and beauty. As the largest ship ever built, Titanic had to be sturdy enough to easily navigate the North Atlantic's rough seas; but as the finest ship ever built, Titanic had to surpass even the wealthiest passenger's expectations of opulence.

Titanic took shape under the world's largest gantry at Harland & Wolff's Queens Island shipyard. More than 10,000 men worked nearly three years to construct the Ship's hull and internal structure. The hull literally grew up from the ground, where first the keel and bottom plates were laid, followed by the ribs, internal girders, and finally the exterior steel plates.

Overhead, cranes maneuvered many of the huge steel slabs into place, where over three million rivets secured them together. Harland & Wolff mainly employed new hydraulic riveting methods, but still used an older, hand-hammering technique for parts of the Ship that were difficult to reach. Crews used steel rivets with the hydraulic riveter and more malleable iron rivets when hand-hammering. This difference in materials may have made some rivets weaker than others.

Several changes needed to be made to Harland & Wolff's Belfast Yards to accommodate the construction of the massive sister ships Olympic and Titanic. Among the changes was the need to build two huge new slipways, which began construction in 1907. Three smaller slips were torn apart and then consolidated into two large slips—slip No.'s 2 and 3—that provided enough space to construct both ships side-by-side. The ground in the new slips was also covered with up to four-and-a-half feet of concrete. In 1908, a gigantic gantry that was also necessary

泰坦尼克号停靠在南安普顿码头 /
Titanic at the wharf in Southampton

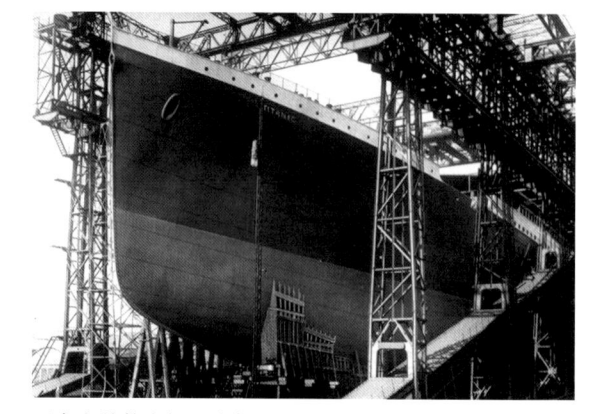

下水之前的泰坦尼克船头 /
The bow of Titanic, prior to its launch

司炉工在为船的锅炉添煤 /
Firemen stoking the ship's boilers

was erected. The completed structure was 70 meters high and weighed about 6,100 metric tons, and was equipped with four large electric lifts as well as a system of cranes.

Harland & Wolff purchased a 200-ton floating crane from Germany that could lift the engines, boilers, and funnels that would be added to both Olympic and *Titanic*. The trench that ran along the line of both ships' launch in front of Victoria Wharf also had to be modified. The trench was originally designed for a depth of 4.5 meters at spring's high tides—this had to be dredged to a depth of 15 meters, and the structure of the wharf also had to be strengthened to accommodate the two huge liners.

On May 31, 1911, a crowd of more than 100,000 gathered to watch *Titanic's* launch. At 12:13 p.m., a red rocket streaked into the sky and the hydraulic triggers holding *Titanic* in its dry dock were released. The sliding way beneath the Ship—greased with 22 tons of tallow and soap—offered no resistance as *Titanic* glided gracefully into the River Lagan amid the congratulatory sounds of ship sirens and a general gasp of wonder from onlookers on both sides of the river. Although she was now in the water, *Titanic* was far from complete: the interior was not finished, and the Ship's engines, boilers, propellers, and four funnels awaited installation. Finishing *Titanic* would take another ten months.

Following her launch, *Titanic* was still an empty shell. For the next

泰坦尼克在贝尔法斯特港下水后 / *Titanic* in Belfast immediately after its launch

ten months, over 3,000 carpenters, engineers, electricians, plumbers, painters, master mechanics, interior designers and craftsmen of every discipline toiled to fit the *Titanic* with latest marine technology and the most sumptuous fixtures and furniture. The Ship's funnels were put in place, as well as much of her machinery and all of her fine appointments.

During her outfitting, *Titanic's* owners reduced the Ship's thirty-two lifeboats to sixteen, the amount required by British law. Although four additional collapsible canvas lifeboats were also added, White Star Line's decision only provided a means of escape for about one-third of the Ship's total capacity.

Titanic sailed out of Belfast Harbor on the evening of April 2, 1912. Earlier that day, the Ship had been subjected to a strenuous sea trial, including an order to reverse its engines while at high speed. At 8 p.m., *Titanic* left the great industrial city of her birth and headed for Southampton, her massive engines rumbling as she steamed down the River Lagan and entered the Irish Sea. Throughout the night, the mighty Ship maintained a steady speed of eighteen knots while her Marconi Wireless sent celebratory messages without cease. Due to freak atmospheric conditions, some of *Titanic's* transmissions were received as far as 4,800 kilometers away.

On Wednesday, April 10, 1912, an air of excitement spread along the docks in Southampton, England. In the early morning, *Titanic's* crew began to board the ship and take up their stations. Many second and third class passengers arrived on a train from London at 9:30 a.m., while most first class passengers arrived in more leisurely fashion aboard the 11:30 a.m. train and were greeted with celebratory music played by the Ship's orchestra. Moments before noon, *Titanic* began her maiden voyage across the North Atlantic for New York.

泰坦尼克号在龙门支架下，贝尔法斯特港 /
Titanic in the gantry at Belfast with a sailing ship in the foreground

贝尔法斯特皇后岛的造船厂工人归家途中 /
Shipyard workers going home from Queen's Island, Belfast

铆钉工在靠近船头区域工作 / Hand-riveters at work near the bow

船体部件

螺旋桨

- 中心螺旋桨有4个叶片，直径5.18米,锰铜铸造，重40000千克。
- 两个侧面的螺旋桨分别有3个叶片，直径7米，每个重68000千克。
- 中心螺旋桨由涡轮机驱动。
- 两个侧面的螺旋桨由两个往复式引擎的蒸汽驱动。

锅炉

- 往复式引擎和涡轮机的动力来自于29个锅炉的蒸汽。
- 每个锅炉高4.5米。
- 锅炉共有159个火炉。

电

- 船上发电设备有4个引擎，位于船尾涡轮机房。
- 电设备动力来自锅炉。
- 发电设备为照明、供暖和机械供电。
- 发电设备位于船尾。
- 试想如果泰坦尼克号船上没有照明会有多么混乱！真正的英雄正是这些锅炉工和修理工，他们坚守岗位，不断地为锅炉填煤，尽可能长时间地延续船上的能源供应。勇敢的工程师同样坚守岗位，以保证船体持续供电。只有通过他们的牺牲才能持续供电。据幸存者回忆，直到最后一刻还看见船上灯火通明。

冷藏

- 船上冷藏有两种用途：
   1) 为乘客提供草莓、花、新鲜水果、冷却饮用水以及其他物资等；
   2) 在欧洲至美国之间运输肉类和水果，从而提供一部分收入。
- 制冷由一个巨大的海水自供制冷系统提供。

锚

- 船上有3只锚。
- 2只锚分别在船头的两侧，每个重14000千克。
- 第3只锚安装在船头甲板上。
- 第3只锚重达28000千克。

船上的锅炉建造当中 /
The ship's boilers during construction

PARTS OF THE *TITANIC*

Propellers

- A central four-bladed propeller with a diameter of 5.18 meters and cast of manganese bronze and weighed 40000kg.
- Two side propellers with three blades with a diameter of 7 m each and weight of 68000kg each.
- The central propeller was powered by a turbine.
- The two side propellers were powered by steam that ran two reciprocating engines.

Boilers

- The reciprocating engines and turbine were powered by steam from twenty-nine boilers.
- Each boiler was 4.5 meters high.
- The boilers fed 159 furnaces.

Electricity

- A generating plant on board had four engines located aft of the turbine engine room.
  - The plant was powered by steam from the boilers.
  - The plant provided electricity for lighting, heating, machinery, etc.
  - The generating plant was located in the stern of the Ship.
  - Imagine the increased chaos on *Titanic* if there had been no electrical lights! The true heroes here are the firemen, stokers, and trimmers who stayed at their posts continuing to feed the huge boilers so that the Ship would retain power as long as possible. In addition, brave engineers also stayed at their posts in the generating plant to ensure that electricity continued to power the lights. Only through their sacrifice did the lights stay on. Survivors recall that the last they saw of the Ship was her lights finally flickering out.

在干船坞的泰坦尼克号的三个螺旋桨 /
A view of *Titanic's* three propellers in dry dock

烟囱

- 泰坦尼克号有4个烟囱。
- 泰坦尼克号只有3个烟囱为发动机排气管，第4个烟囱（假烟囱）用于甲板下的通风。
- 椭圆形烟囱高19米，宽6米，长7米。

汽笛

- 4个3风铃汽笛分别安装在4个烟囱上。
- 每套汽笛有大、中、小3个铃，同时吹响时会发出悠扬的声音。
- 只有前面2个烟囱上的两2汽笛是可以使用的，另外2套只是为了设计对称装饰。

被载运在马车上经过贝尔法斯特街道的泰坦尼克号船锚 /
Titanic's anchor being pulled by horse-drawn carriage through the streets of Belfast

泰坦尼克号上的救生艇 / Lifeboats aboard *Titanic*

Refrigeration

- Refrigeration on *Titanic* served two purposes:
  1) To be able to provide strawberries, flowers, fresh fruits, cooled drinking water, and other provisions to passengers;
  2) To provide a stream of revenue in transport of commercial shipments of meats, fruits, etc, between Europe and the USA.
- Refrigeration was provided by a large self-sustaining brine refrigeration system.

Anchors

- *Titanic* had 3 anchors.
- There were two anchors on each side of the bow. Each one weighed 14000kg.
- The third anchor was stowed on the bow deck.
- The third anchor weighed 28000kg.

Funnels

- *Titanic* had four funnels.
- *Titanic* used only three funnels for engine exhaust. The fourth or 'fake' funnel provided ventilation from below decks.
- The oval-shaped funnels measured 19 meters high, 6 meters wide, and 7 meters long.

Whistles

- The four three-chime whistle sets were attached one to each of the four funnels.
- Each set had a small, medium, and large sized whistles, when blown together they made a melodious sound.
- Only the sets on the first two funnels were functional, the whistle sets of funnels three and four were non-functional and were used only for design symmetry.

内部装潢

登上泰坦尼克号

- 泰坦尼克号前往纽约的头等船票需花费2500美金，大约相当于今天的57200美金。两间最豪华最昂贵的套房位于B层甲板，价格高达4500美金，大约等于今天的103000美金。
- 1张泰坦尼克号的三等舱船票是40美金，大约相当于今天的900美金。每间三等船舱可居住多达10人，按男女性别划分，所以很多家庭被分在不同船舱。
- 头等舱乘客享用船上付费休闲娱乐：游泳池票价25美分，壁球场门票（也为专业球员提供服务）50美分。
- 泰坦尼克号上的5间厨房有60名厨师和厨师助理，负责熬汤、烧烤、烘焙和蔬菜烹制。还有1位犹太教的厨师，专门为犹太乘客准备膳食。
- 泰坦尼克号船上拥有自己的报纸《大西洋日报》。除了新闻报道和广告，报纸上还有每天的菜单、最新股价、赛马结果和社会八卦新闻。
- 船上只给700多名三等舱乘客配置了两个浴缸。
- 船上为住在甲板前部的一等舱和住在甲板后部的部分二等舱乘客配置了散步空间。因此这两个舱位的人最有机会登上救生艇，因为他们可以快速、轻松地登上救生艇。

大楼梯

毫无疑问，大楼梯在泰坦尼克号上是最引人注目的。大楼梯设在轮船前端，从救生艇甲板延伸至客舱甲板之间，使得头等舱乘客可以轻松、优雅地穿过轮船的上层甲板。楼梯的顶部是一个镶嵌了彩色玻璃的拱形铁穹，自然光能够透过并覆盖楼梯第一个平台，平台上镶嵌了一块加冕时代"荣耀时刻"图案的精美雕刻嵌板。

大楼梯上手持电力照明火炬的天使像 / A cherub holding an electrically illuminated torch in the Grand Staircase

INTERIOR DECORATION

On Board *Titanic*

- The cost of a first class ticket on *Titanic* to New York was $2,500, approximately $57,200 today. The two most luxurious and expensive suites located on B Deck, however, were a staggering $4,500, approximately $103,000 today.
- A third class ticket on the *Titanic* cost $40, which is approximately $900 in today's currency. Up to ten people resided in third class rooms. The rooms were divided by gender, often times splitting families.
- First class passengers had the luxury of paying for their leisure while on board: a ticket to the swimming pool cost 25¢, while a ticket for the squash court (as well as the services of a professional player) cost 50¢.
- Sixty chefs and chefs' assistants worked in the *Titanic's* five kitchens. They ranged from soup and roast cooks to pastry chefs and vegetable cooks. There was also a kosher cook to prepare the meals for the Jewish passengers.
- *Titanic* had its own newspaper, the Atlantic Daily Bulletin, prepared aboard the Ship. In addition to news articles and advertisements, it contained a daily menu, the latest stock prices, horse-racing results, and society gossip.
- There were only two bathtubs for the more than 700 third class passengers aboard the Ship.
- The forward part of the Boat Deck was promenade space for first class passengers and the rear part for second class passengers. People from these classes thus had the best chance of getting into a lifeboat, simply because they could get to them quickly and easily.

Grand Staircase

Titanic's Grand Staircase was, without doubt, one of its most spectacular features. Located at the forward end of the Ship, the Grand Staircase extended between the Boat Deck and the Saloon Deck, allowing first class passengers to move through the Ship's upper decks with ease and elegance. The Staircase was topped by a dome of iron and stained glass, which allowed natural light to fill the first landing where an elaborately carved panel featured the figures of Honor and Glory crowning Time.

大楼梯 /
A view of the Grand Staircase

À la Carte餐厅

À la Carte餐厅位于船桥甲板上，与其说是为头等舱乘客提供奢华的食物，倒不如说是一种奢华的就餐体验。À la Carte餐厅的特点是，其专业服务员均来自伦敦著名的Luigi Gatti 餐厅，而且在食物、服务及装饰方面是船上所有餐厅中最好的。头等舱船票价格不包含在À la Carte就餐的费用内。但是，白星航运公司为那些选择在该餐厅就餐的乘客提供了小金额的报销退款。

头等舱 À la Carte 餐厅 / The First Class À la Carte Restaurantt

头等舱吸烟室

头等舱吸烟室设在散步长廊甲板上，为头等舱男性乘客专用。这间房间的中部是一个大型、华丽的壁炉，头等舱男性乘客在晚餐后会聚集在这里，享用雪茄、法国白兰地，享受交流的快乐。通过近船尾的旋转门，可以从吸烟室进入露天阳台咖啡馆和棕榈阁。

头等舱阅览室

吸烟室是专为头等舱先生们准备的，而阅览及写作室则是为泰坦尼克号头等舱的女士们专门设计的。在这里，女士们可以阅读最喜爱的小说，或者给家人和朋友写信。其他人则可在炉火前放松休憩，通过大型凸窗欣赏头等舱散步长廊和一望无际的北大西洋。

阳台咖啡馆

阳台咖啡馆设在A甲板头等舱吸烟室的后面。咖啡馆的特色设计包括：差不多2.1米高的青铜框拱窗，可使大量室外阳光照进室内，营造室外露台的效果。因为在窗前种植棕榈树，所以这个地方有时也被乘客们称为棕榈阁。头等舱乘客的孩子们经常把咖啡馆当作游乐区，在格子图案的地板上追逐。

阳台咖啡馆 / The Verandah Café

头等舱吸烟室 /
First Class Smoking Room

头等舱阅览室 / First Class Reading and Writing Room

À la Carte Restaurant

The À la Carte Restaurant located on the Bridge Deck, offered *Titanic's* first class passengers an even more lavish dining experience than the sumptuous fare in the First Class Dining Salon.. Featuring an expert waitstaff from London's famous Luigi Gatti Restaurant, the À la Carte Restaurant boasted the finest food, service, and décor of any dining room afloat. Meals at the À la Carte Restaurant were not included with the price of a first class ticket. White Star Line did, however, offer a modest reimbursement for those passengers choosing to dine at the restaurant.

First Class Smoking Room

Located on the Promenade Deck, the First Class Smoking Room was intended for the exclusive use of first class male passengers. The central feature of this room was a large, ornate fireplace around which first class male passengers would gather after dinner to enjoy cigars, cognac, and conversation. Revolving doors led from the smoking room to the open-air Verandah Café and Palm Court.

First Class Reading Room

While the Smoking Room was intended for the men of First Class, the Reading and Writing Room was designed for *Titanic's* first class ladies. Here the ladies of the Ship could read a favorite novel or write letters to friends and family. Others could relax by the fire while looking through the room's large bay window to the First Class Promenade and the endless horizon of the North Atlantic.

The Verandah Café

The Verandah Café was located on A Deck just behind the First Class Smoking Room. The Café featured bronze-framed, arched windows that were nearly seven feet tall, allowing large amounts of light to filter into the room and creating an outdoor patio effect. Palm trees stood in front of the windows, and the area was sometimes referred to by passengers as the Palm Court. Children of first class passengers were often seen using the Café as a play area, scurrying about on the checkered floor.

土耳其浴室

土耳其浴室是泰坦尼克号上最奢华的区域之一，只供头等舱乘客使用。设计人员绞尽脑汁，力图使土耳其浴室看上去具有浓厚的"异国"情调——东方风情。使用泰坦尼克号的土耳其浴室不是免费的，浴室票可从轮船的问询处购买，每人4个英国先令或1美元。

健身房

泰坦尼克号拥有一个设备精良的健身房，供头等舱舱使用。该健身房有两个划船健身器、一个自行车比赛机、一台骑马机，甚至还设有一个旋转机（也称电动骆驼）。此外还配有背部和腹部按摩机，而且壁球爱好者可按1美元每半小时的单价享用壁球室。那些热衷于水中运动的人可在轮船的泳池里游上几个来回。健身设施每天向乘客的开放时间为上午10点到下午6点，对儿童开放的时间为下午1点到3点。

巴黎咖啡馆

巴黎咖啡馆位于À la Carte餐厅外面，头等舱乘客可以享用与餐厅相同的菜品，但咖啡馆的环境却别具一格，看起来像沐浴在阳光下的阳台。朋友和家人在餐厅用餐前喜欢在此聚会。大型观景窗让海景尽收眼底。天气好时，巴黎咖啡馆会摇下窗户，让乘客们享受户外用餐的体验。

散步甲板

散步甲板，也称甲板A，专供头等舱乘客享用。该甲板是轮船两侧150米长的散步长廊。在这里，头等舱乘客会坐在折叠式躺椅上，或悠闲地漫步，同时欣赏海景，与同行乘客交流。散步甲板的露天区域也是头等舱乘客的小孩的最爱。他们露天玩耍，或从轮船的一端跑到另一端。

头等舱客舱

泰坦尼克号可容纳750多名头等舱乘客。所有头等舱都很大，在材料及工艺方面，可与全球最好的酒店相媲美。宽敞的壁橱、配有全浴缸的私人浴室，以及冷热自来水都是标准配置。很多头等舱舱室都与会客室相邻，两间最豪华的套房位于甲板B处，还设有私人散步长廊。

健身房 / The Gymnasium

头等舱客舱 / First Class Stateroom

Turkish Baths

One of the most opulent areas onboard *Titanic* was the Turkish Baths, which were for the exclusive use of first class passengers. Much effort was put into making the Turkish Baths as "exotic" looking as possible, i.e. "eastern." Use of *Titanic's* Turkish Baths was not free and tickets could be purchased from the Ship's enquiry office for four British shillings, or one US dollar, per person.

Gymnasium

Titanic offered a well-equipped gymnasium for the use of her first class passengers. The gymnasium featured two rowing machines, a bicycle-racing machine, a horse-riding machine, and even a trunk-rotating machine (also called an electric camel). Back and stomach massage machines were also available, and racquet enthusiasts could pay $1.00 per half hour to enjoy the squash court. Those seeking aquatic exercise could swim several laps in the Ship's pool. The fitness facilities were open each day from 10 a.m. to 6 p.m. for ladies and men and children were allowed in the gymnasium from 1:00 p.m. to 3:00 p.m.

Café Parisien

Situated outside the À la Carte Restaurant , the Café Parisien allowed first-class passengers to be served the same meals as inside the restaurant, but in a setting that gave the appearance of a sun-drenched verandah. It was also a popular meeting place for friends and family members before being seated in the restaurant. Large picture windows afforded diners a fine view of the sea, and in good weather the windows of the Café Parisien could be rolled down, allowing passengers to dine al fresco.

Promenade Deck

The Promenade Deck, or A Deck, was dedicated solely to the enjoyment of first class passengers. The principal feature of this deck, however, was its promenade, which extended for 500 feet on either side of the Ship. Here, first class passengers could sit in deck chairs or take a gentle stroll while enjoying sweeping vistas of the sea and mingling with their fellow passengers. The Promenade Deck's long expanse was a favorite of first class children as well; they were often seen playing in the open air or racing from one end of the Ship to the other.

First Class Cabin

Titanic could accommodate over 750 first class passengers. All first-class cabins were exceptionally large, offering fine materials and craftsmanship that rivaled that of the world's finest hotels. Abundant closet space, private baths with full bathtubs, and hot and cold running water were standard. Many first class staterooms also featured adjoining parlor rooms, while the two most luxurious suites, located on B Deck, included private promenades.

头等舱散步甲板 / First Class Promenade

头等舱客舱 / First Class Stateroom

二等舱便利设施

泰坦尼克号的二等舱客舱可与同时代很多其他远洋班轮的头等舱客舱相媲美,而且成本几乎相差无几。用橡木装饰的轮船二等舱餐厅设在客舱甲板上,一次可同时容纳394名乘客。因此,乘客们可在这个十七世纪装饰风格的空间里分批享受用餐服务。因为头等舱与二等舱的厨房合在一起,所以泰坦尼克号二等舱乘客的餐饮几乎与头等舱乘客是相同级别。

三等舱

乘坐泰坦尼克号旅行的三等舱乘客主要是到美国追求更美好生活的欧洲移民。有些人已经在美国定居,探亲后返回。有些人的家属已经移民美国,此次旅行的费用由美国家属提供。有些乘客能够支付得起二等舱船票,但是想节省前往美国的费用。三等舱可能会住着多达四种不同语言的陌生人。

客舱非常狭窄,而且设计简单。天花板覆盖有一堆管道与支撑梁,而且总能听到和感觉到发动机的噪音与震动声。虽然存在这些不利条件,但很多三等舱乘客发现他们的住房很大。不像其他班轮用稻草作为床垫,泰坦尼克号的铺位配有真正的床垫。

二等舱客舱 / Second Class Stateroom

船员居住设施

根据泰坦尼克号的设计要求,应最大限度地实现乘客与船员的隔离。乘客除了与餐厅人员、甲板服务员及高级船员的相互接触外,白星航运公司煞费苦心,使乘客完全看不到其他船员。身上较脏的工程部人员住在轮船前部的宿舍中,有些房间最多可容纳50人。船员也有独立的通道穿过轮船。轮机部船员通过靠近船首的螺旋梯与通往锅炉房下面的通道报到上班。

二等舱餐厅 / Second Class Dining Saloon

乘客在二等舱散步甲板 / Passenger on the Second Class Promenade

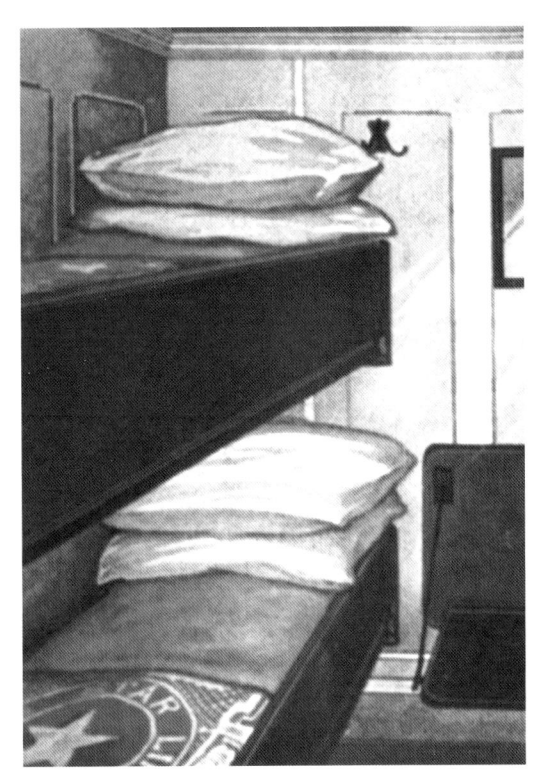

三等舱客舱 / Third Class Cabin

Second Class Amenities

Titanic's second class cabins were comparable to first class cabins on many other ocean liners of the era, and cost nearly as much. The Ship's oak-paneled Second Class Dining Saloon, located on the Saloon Deck, could accommodate 394 passengers at a time. For this reason, meals in the seventeenth-century-styled room were served in sittings. Because the first and second class galleys were combined, *Titanic's* second class passengers ate nearly as well as their counterparts in first class.

Third Class

Third class passengers traveling on *Titanic* were mostly European immigrants looking for a better life in America. Some had already established themselves in the United States and were returning after visits home. Others were joining family members who had traveled ahead of them and had sent money for their journey. Some passengers may have been able to afford a second class ticket but wanted to save money for their arrival in America. A third class cabin would likely be occupied by up to four strangers who spoke different languages.

Cabins were cramped and very plain in design. The ceilings were covered with a tangle of pipes and support beams, and the noise and vibration of the engines could always be heard and felt. Despite these conditions, many third class passengers found their accommodations to be more than adequate. Unlike other liners, which used straw, *Titanic's* bunks had real mattresses.

Crew Accommodations

Titanic's design called for maximum separation of passengers and crew. Apart from expected interactions with dining room staff, deck stewards, and officers, White Star Line took great pains to keep the rest of the crew completely invisible. The dirtier crew members of the engineering department were quartered in dormitories at the front of the Ship. Some rooms held up to fifty men. Crew members also had separate routes to travel through the Ship. The engine crew reported to work via spiral staircases close to the bow and through a tunnel that ran beneath the boiler rooms.

三等舱餐厅 / Third Class Dining Saloon

货物清单

清单来自白星航运公司办公室,为标准的商业清单,总价值相当于约1千万美金(2015年)。

部分货物:

泰坦尼克号的食物

1. 新鲜肉类:75000 磅
2. 鲜鱼:11000 磅
3. 培根和火腿:7500 磅
4. 新鲜鸡蛋:40000 个
5. 冰淇淋:1750 夸脱
6. 咖啡:2200 磅
7. 茶:800 磅
8. 面粉:200 桶
9. 橘子:36000 个
10. 柠檬:16000 个
11. 新鲜牛奶:1500 加仑
12. 黄油:6000 磅
13. 番茄:2¾ 吨
14. 土豆:40 吨
15. 啤酒和烈性黑啤:20000 瓶
16. 葡萄酒:1500 瓶
17. 烈性酒:850 瓶
18. 香槟:63 箱

泰坦尼克号的食物用具

1. 茶杯:3000 个
2. 晚餐碟子:12000 个
3. 冰淇淋盘:5500 个
4. 舒芙蕾盘子:1500 个
5. 酒杯:2000 个
6. 盐瓶:2000 个
7. 布丁盘子:1200 个
8. 手指碗:1000 个
9. 牡蛎叉:1000 只
10. 核桃夹:300 个
11. 鸡蛋勺:2000 条
12. 葡萄剪刀:1500 把
13. 芦笋钳:400 把

泰坦尼克号的货物

1. 700 到 800 个包裹,装有 3364 袋信件。
2. 威廉·卡特乘客的 1 辆 35 马力雷诺汽车。
3. 埃德温娜·特劳特乘客的 1 台果酱机。
4. 帕克蒂尔福德的 1 箱牙膏。
5. 3 箱皂用香料。
6. 8 箱兰花。
7. 11 捆纽约州国家城市银行的橡胶。
8. 1 桶运往蒂芙尼的瓷器。
9. 34 件斯伯丁的运动用品。
10. 1本珠宝版的奥玛·珈音著《鲁拜集》,艾力库·维达插图。该书于1912年3月以405镑拍卖给一名美国人。该册书花了两年装订,由1050颗珍贵宝石装饰,每一颗都用黄金镶嵌。
11. 4 箱鸦片。

TITANIC CARGO MANIFEST LIST

This is taken from a copy of the manifest at White Star Line Offices. It is a standard commercial list with a total value of approximately $10 million USD in 2015.

Part of the manifest list:

Titanic's Food

Fresh Meat: 75,000 lbs

Fresh Fish: 11,000 lbs

Bacon and Ham: 7,500 lbs

Fresh Eggs: 40,000

Ice Cream: 1,750 qts

Coffee: 2,200 lbs

Tea: 800 lbs

Flour: 200 barrels

Oranges: 36,000

Lemons: 16,000

Fresh Milk: 1,500 gallons

Butter: 6,000 lbs

Tomatoes: 2¾ tons

Potatoes: 40 tons

Beer and Stout: 20,000 bottles

Wines: 1,500 bottles

Spirits: 850 bottles

Champagne: 63 cases

Titanic's Serving Utensils

Tea Cups: 3,000

Dinner Plates: 12,000

Ice Cream Plates: 5,500

Soufflé Dishes: 1,500

Wine Glasses: 2,000

Salt Shakers: 2,000

Pudding Dishes: 1,200

Finger Bowls: 1,000

Oyster Forks: 1,000

Nut Crackers: 300

Egg Spoons: 2,000

Grape Scissors: 1,500

Asparagus Tongs: 400

Cargo: The Usual and Unusual

1. 3,364 bags of mail on board and 700-800 parcels.
2. One Renault 35 hp automobile owned by passenger William Carter.
3. One Marmalade Machine owned by passenger Edwina Trout.
4. One Case of toothpaste for Park & Tilford.
5. Three Cases of Soap Perfume.
6. Eight Cases of Orchids.
7. Eleven bales of rubber for the National City Bank of New York.
8. A cask of china headed for Tiffany's was in the cargo hold.
9. Thirty-four cases of athletic goods for A.G. Spalding.
10. A jewelled copy of The Rubáiyát by Omar Khayyám, with illustrations by Eliku Vedder sold for 405 at auction in March of 1912 to an American bidder. The binding took two years to execute, and the decoration embodied 1,050 precious stones, each separately set in gold.
11. Four cases of opium.

船员信息

高级船员
船长 Edward J. Smith： 月薪 105 英镑
乘务长 Henry Wilde：月薪 25 英镑
大副 William M. Murdoch
二副 Charles Lightoller
三副 Herbert Pitman
四副 Joseph Boxhall
五副 Harold Lowe
六副 James Moody

瞭望员
六名瞭望员，每两名一组轮班。
当发现冰山时，瞭望员 Frederick Fleet 和 Reginald Lee 在瞭望台值班。
每名瞭望员月薪为 5 英镑 5 先令。

Smith 船长和其他泰坦尼克号上的高级船员。
后排从左至右分别是：
事务长 McElroy、二副 Lightoller、三副 Pitman、四副 Boxhall、五副 Lowe。
前排从左至右分别是：
六副 Moody、大副 Henry Wilde、船长 Smith 和大副 Murdoch。

Capitain Smith and his officers on board.
Left to right on the back row:
McElroy, Lightoller, Pitman, Boxhall and Lowe.
Left to right on the front row:
Moody, Henry Wilde, Smith and Murdoch.

CREW MEMBERS

Smith 船长 / Capitain Smith

Frederick Fleet 瞭望员 / Frederick Fleet (Lookout)

Officers

Captain Edward J. Smith (monthly wage £105)

Chief Officer Henry Wilde (monthly wage £25)

First Officer William M. Murdoch

Second Officer Charles Lightoller

Third Officer Herbert Pitman

Fourth Officer Joseph Boxall

Fifth Officer Harold Lowe

Sixth Officer James Moody

Lookouts

There were six lookouts who took their watches in pairs.

Lookouts Frederick Fleet and Reginald Lee were on duty in the crow's nest and were the first to sight the iceberg.

Each received a monthly pay of £5 plus 5 shillings as lookout.

舵手

泰坦尼克号船上有 7 名舵手。

舵手负责掌舵、控制船、航行和船桥值班。

泰坦尼克号撞击冰山时，舵手 Robert Hichens 负责掌舵。

舵手平均月薪为 5 英镑。

一级水手

一级水手经过特殊训练，要求高于普通水手。

泰坦尼克号船上有 30 名一级水手。

每艘救生艇上安排 1 名一级水手。

一级水手月薪为 5 英镑。

工程部：工程师、修理工、锅炉工和电工

工程部有 326 名工作人员。

包括 33 名工程师，负责操作和维修机械设备。

每个锅炉有 3 个火炉，锅炉工负责为火炉填煤。

餐饮部：乘务员、厨师等

事务长全权负责餐饮部工作，是乘客和船员之间的直接纽带。

该部有男、女工作人员 421 名，为乘客提供服务。

膳务长 Charles J. Joughin 月薪为 12 英镑。

销售部

À la carte 餐厅人员：

该餐厅为 Luigi Gatti 先生经营的私营特许餐厅。

工作人员包括厨师、服务员、清洁工，由 Gatti 先生支付工资。

餐厅提供特殊餐饮服务。

职员多为意大利人或法国人。

泰坦尼克号乐师 / Musicians of the *Titan*

Quartermasters

There were seven quartermasters on *Titanic*.

A quartermaster serves as helmsman and performs ship control, navigation and bridge watch duties.

Quartermaster Robert Hichens was at the helm when *Titanic* struck the iceberg.

The average monthly wage for a quartermaster was £5.

Able-Bodied Seamen

An able-bodied seaman has received specialized training above that or an ordinary seaman.

There were thirty able bodied seamen on *Titanic*.

Each ABS was assigned to a lifeboat.

The monthly wage was £5.

Engineering Department: Engineers, Trimmers, Firemen, Electricians

There were 326 men in the engineering department.

Included in this group were thirty-three engineers who operated and maintained the mechanical equipment.

The firemen ensured that the three furnaces on each boiler were filled with coal.

Victualling Department: Stewards, cooks, etc.

The Purser supervised all of the Victualling Department and was the direct link between passengers and officers.

421 men and women in this department worked directly with passengers.

Chief Baker Charles J. Joughin had a monthly wage of £12.

Vendor Department

À la carte Restaurant personnel:

The restaurant was a private concession managed by Mr. Luigi Gatti.

The staff included cooks, waiters, and clean up staff all paid by Mr. Gatti as the restaurant received separate payment for meals.

The staff were primarily Italian or French nationals.

理发师

船上有 3 名理发师,分别为三个等级的客舱服务。他们只赚取小费。

邮政人员

船上有 5 名邮政人员:3 名为美国邮政局工作,2 名则为皇家邮政局工作人员。他们在邮政局工作,负责对发往纽约的邮件进行分类。

乐队

8 名音乐师受聘于利物浦 C.W. 和 F.N. Black 公司。

他们为二等舱乘客,而非乘务人员。

音乐师分为三重奏组和五重奏组。

他们的月薪为 4 英镑以及小费。

无线电通讯员

船上有 2 名通讯员:Jack Phillips 和 Harold Bride。

月薪为 2 英镑 2 先令 6 便士。

通讯员受聘于马可尼国际海上通讯有限公司。

他们身穿马可尼公司服装,不属于普通乘务人员。

他们的主要工作是为付费乘客收发信息。

无线电发报员

Phillips 和 Bride

John George "Jack" Phillips(电报员)/
John George "Jack" Phillips (Telegraphist)

Harold Sydney Bride（助理电报员）/
Harold Sydney Bride (Assistant Telegraphist)

Barbers

There were three barbers on board, one for each class of service. They worked for tips only.

Postal Service Clerks

There were five postal clerks: three employed by the U.S. Post Office and two employed by the Royal Post Office

The clerks operated a post office and spent time sorting the mail for distribution in New York.

Musicians

The eight musicians were employed by the C.W. and F.N. Black Company of Liverpool;

They travelled as second class passengers, not as part of the crew;

The musicians were divided into a trio and a quintet;

They had a monthly wage of £4 plus tips.

Marconi Radio Operators

There were two radio operators: Jack Phillips and Harold Bride;

Monthly wage was £2, 2 shillings, and six pence ;

The operators were employees of the Marconi International Marine Communication Company, Ltd.;

They wore Marconi uniforms and were not considered part of the regular crew;

Their primary job was to send and receive messages paid for by passengers.

Marconi Radio Operators

Phillips and Bride

问题释疑

多少位生还者今天还在世？

最后一位生还者米莉维娜·迪恩于 2009 年 5 月 31 日离世，享年 97 岁。

泰坦尼克号可以被打捞上来吗？

遗憾的是，尽管现有科技可以将沉船从海底打捞上来，但是沉船太脆弱，无法承受被举起和运输。

哪些船赶来救援，哪些没有？

灾难发生当晚收到泰坦尼克号求救信号的船只包括：卡帕提亚、圣殿山、弗吉尼亚州、波罗的海、卡罗尼亚、弗里德里希威廉亲王、法兰克福和泰坦尼克号的姐妹船奥林匹克号。一开始，其中几条船都改变航线驶向撞击地点，但是发现显然只有卡帕提亚能在适当的时间内赶到事发地点时，他们又重新继续原来的航线。有一条船，莱兰海运的加利福尼亚号距离泰坦尼克号只有几英里，但加利福尼亚号当天晚上在浮冰里停留，因为船长认为在晚上穿越冰原太危险。尽管加利福尼亚号安装了无线电设备，但由于接线员晚上睡觉了，所以错过了遇险信息。在今天看来，加利福尼亚号甲板船员没有积极调查看到的远处火箭与灯光，这是否属于失职，仍存有很大争议。

为什么泰坦尼克号没有装载足够的救生艇？

泰坦尼克号的救生艇数量须遵循英国贸易委员会 1894 年起草的规则。到 1912 年，这些救生艇规定已经严重过时。泰坦尼克号救生艇的数量超过法规要求的 4 倍。根据法律，不管船上的实际人数有多少，都无需携带超过 16 艘救生艇。当泰坦尼克号离开南安普敦时，它实际携带了比法律要求还多的数量：16 艘救生艇和另外 4 艘可折叠艇。造船业意识到救生艇规则很快就会修改，因此白星公司设计了足够的甲板空间和吊艇柱以满足"所有人都有艇"的原则。但是在法律真正更改以前，他们并不打算安装。这个决定在今天看起来难以理解，但是在 1912 年，人们对待灾难预防的态度完全不同。在 20 世纪之初，船主们非常不愿意携带超过法定最低数量的救生艇，因为它们会占用一等舱和二等舱甲板的大量空间。而且，救生艇购买和维护的费用都很昂贵，还会影响船只的稳定性。在泰坦尼克号灾难发生前的几年，人们还认为配置大量救生艇意味着船不安全。非常奇怪的是，在 20 世纪 50 年代汽车安装安全带时，人们同样表现出不情愿。汽车制造商不愿意在车上安装安全带，因为他们觉得安全带似乎意味着汽车不安全。

2010 年水下探险考察到的泰坦尼克号 /
A view of *Titanic* underwater during a 2010 expedition to the wreck site

FREQUENTLY ASKED QUESTIONS

J. Bruce Ismay 在贸易局听证会上作证 /
J. Bruce Ismay testifying before the Board of Trade Inquiry

童子军为泰坦尼克受灾基金募集 /
Boyscouts fundraising for the *Titanic* Disaster Fund

How many survivors are alive today?

The last living survivor, Millvina Dean, recently passed away on May 31, 2009 as the oldest survivor of *Titanic* at age 97.

Can Titanic *be raised?*

Sadly, even if the technology existed to raise it from the seabed, the wreck is far too fragile to withstand lifting and transportation.

What ships came to Titanic's *rescue and what ships did not?*

Titanic's distress call was received by several ships the night of the disaster including the Carpathia, Mount Temple, Virginian, Baltic, Caronia, Prinz Fredrich Wilhelm, Frankfurt and the *Titanic*'s sister ship the Olympic. Initially, several of these ships altered course towards the collision site, but when it became apparent that Carpathia alone would make it to the scene of the accident in reasonable time, they resumed their previous courses. One ship, the Leyland Line's Californian was only a few miles distant from the *Titanic*. The Californian had stopped for the night because her Captain felt it too dangerous to proceed through the ice field in the dark. Although fitted with wireless, the Californian's operator had turned in for the night and missed the distress call. To this day, there is considerable controversy as to whether the Californian's deck officers were negligent in not making a more aggressive investigation into rockets and lights seen in the distance.

Why didn't Titanic *carry enough lifeboats?*

Titanic's lifeboat capacity was governed by the British Board of Trade's rules, which were drafted in 1894. By 1912, these lifeboat regulations were badly out of date. The *Titanic* was four times larger than the largest legal classification considered under these rules and by law was not required to carry more than sixteen lifeboats, regardless of the actual number of people onboard. When she left Southampton, *Titanic* actually carried more than the law required: sixteen lifeboats and four additional collapsible boats. The shipping industry was aware that the lifeboat regulations were going to be changed soon and *Titanic*'s deck space and davits were designed for the anticipated "boats for all" policy, but until the law actually changed, White Star was not going to install them. The decision seems difficult to understand today, but in 1912, the attitude towards accident prevention was much different. At the turn of the century, ship owners were reluctant to exceed the legal minimum because lifeboats took up most of the space on first and second class decks. Boats were expensive to purchase, maintain, and affected a ship's stability. Finally, in the years before the *Titanic* disaster, it was felt that the very presence of large numbers of lifeboats suggested that somehow the vessel was unsafe. Oddly, the same reluctance showed up as late as the 1950s for automobile seatbelts. Car makers at that time were also reluctant to install seatbelts because the belts seemed to imply there was something unsafe about the car.

三等舱乘客是被故意留在甲板下面的吗？

英国和美国的调查都显示：尽管三等舱乘客的确在船下沉很久以后才来到甲板上，但是没有证据表明三等舱乘客是被故意留在甲板下面的。合理的解释是船上的高级船员被灾难弄得惊慌失措，忽略了下达疏散三等舱的命令。白星公司没有制定这类事故的应急方案，而船上的高级船员们则忙于应付危机，下放救生艇。为了维持疏散秩序，三等舱乘务员让乘客在下面等待，没有人想到下达命令。

是否只有妇女和儿童被允许登上救生艇？

传统上，妇女和儿童优先上救生艇，男士填补后离开的救生艇。然而，由于泰坦尼克号救生艇的短缺，这个传统意味着伤亡名单上多为男性。在泰坦尼克号的左舷，高级船员莱托勒监管救生艇的下放。他按照字面意思理解这条规定，不允许除了艇上船员之外的任何男性登上救生艇。在泰坦尼克号下沉的初期，因为船看起来完全没有问题，女士们很自然不愿意弃船而去。这导致了很多救生艇没有装满就被放走了。而在船的右舷，高级船员默多克解读这条规则为"妇女和孩子优先上船"——只有当所有女士都得到座位了，附近的男士如果愿意撤离的，才可以上船。

谁该拥有沉船？

根据海事法，船舶的所有者拥有其沉船的所有权，除非所有者放弃沉船或船沉没过后很长时间。人们普遍认为，白星航运公司将公司卖给丘纳德时不包括泰坦尼号邮轮，因为当时邮轮已经沉没而且没有打捞。船体的一部分受保于几家保险公司，但没有任何一家对邮轮提出过所有权。由于被遗弃，到目前为止，没有任何法院将所有权判给另一个实体。

皇家邮轮泰坦尼克公司如何获得了泰坦尼号的打捞占有权？

根据海事法，皇家邮轮泰坦尼克公司于1993年在沉船残骸区域进行文物打捞，并将它们带到弗吉尼亚州诺福克的海事法庭。1994年6月7日，美国弗吉尼亚东区地方法院宣布皇家邮轮泰坦尼克公司拥有对泰坦尼克号沉船和沉船遗址的独家打捞权，不允许其他单位前往沉船遗址进行打捞。皇家邮轮泰坦尼克公司是泰坦尼号沉船打捞和文物保存的唯一实体。

高级船员船舱窗户 / Windows of the Officers' Quarters

Were third-class passengers deliberately kept below decks?

Both the British and American inquiries found that there was no evidence to suggest that third class passengers were deliberately kept below decks, although it is true that third class passengers did not make their way to the Boat Deck until very late in the sinking. A reasonable explanation is that the Ship's officers were overwhelmed by the disaster and simply overlooked sending specific orders to evacuate third class. White Star had formulated no emergency plans for this type of accident and the Ship's officers were fully preoccupied with the crisis and the launch of lifeboats. In an attempt to provide for an orderly evacuation, third class stewards held passengers below waiting for orders that nobody thought to give.

Were only women and children allowed in the lifeboats?

Traditionally, first seats in lifeboats are given to women and children, with men filling up the late leaving lifeboats. However, given *Titanic's* lifeboat shortage, this tradition meant that the casualty list was more heavily male. On the port side of *Titanic*, the lifeboat launchings were supervised by Officer Lightoller, who took this order literally, preventing any men except the boat crews from embarking. Early in the sinking, women were naturally reluctant to abandon a ship that did not seem at all to be in trouble, and as a result, many of these boats were sent away only partially full. On the starboard side, Officer Murdoch interpreted the order to mean "women and children first on deck," and only after all the seats had been offered to women, could any men on hand, who wished to evacuate, do so.

Who owns the wreck?

Under admiralty law, the owner of a ship retains rights to its wreck, unless the owner abandons it or an unusually long period of time has passed since the vessel sank. It is generally accepted when the White Star Line sold their company to Cunard, *Titanic* was not included in the sale because it had sunk and could not be recovered. A portion of the hull was insured by several insurance companies, none of which have ever stepped forward to claim ownership. To date, no court has awarded ownership rights, due to abandonment, to another entity.

How did RMS Titanic, *Inc. (RMST) gain salvor-in-possession rights to* Titanic?

RMST, in compliance with admiralty law, recovered objects from the wreck site in 1993 and brought them into an admiralty court in Norfolk Virginia. On June 7, 1994, the United States District Court for the Eastern District of Virginia declared RMST salvor-in-possession of the wreck and wreck site of the RMS *Titanic*, excluding all others from going to the site for the purpose of recovery. RMST is the only entity that has recovered and conserved items from *Titanic*.

在海底的双耳盘 /Au gratin dishes on the sea floor

电报机出水前 /A telegraph prior to recovery

后 记

泰坦尼克号的沉没是人类历史上的大事件。它包含众多传奇元素，故被赋予无数文化符号。关于泰坦尼克号的各类小说、纪实、电影层出不穷，使得这个西方文明的重大历史事件成为了家喻户晓、常讲常新的话题。1997年好莱坞导演詹姆斯·卡梅隆以影视的手法把这段历史真实地呈现给人们，感动了全球观众。电影《泰坦尼克号》上映以来，一直风靡全球，其中一个重要原因就是，这部电影形象地再现了当年的人类文明。在中国，大多数人也是通过电影对泰坦尼克号有了认识并进行关注。泰坦尼克不仅仅局限于一个故事，而且它本身涵盖了欧美社会政治、经济、文化、社会生活、工业生产的各个方面，由个体视角折射出的想象不可估量。

1912年2月15日凌晨，泰坦尼克号不幸沉入北大西洋距海平面3800米深的海底。沉船于1985年被成功定位，美国普利尔展览公司自1987年就开始全权负责泰坦尼克号的打捞、维护以及研究工作。汉古艺术馆引进该公司精心制作的"泰坦尼克文物精品展"，展出从深海沉船中打捞出水的文物精品300件套，为观众展现那个时代的真实印记。展览还花费重金，将这艘豪华巨轮诸多场景复原，包括船长室、头等舱、豪华大楼梯、咖啡厅、散步长廊、锅炉房等，给了人们身临其境"登上"泰坦尼克号的机会。我们用艺术馆独有的视角和语言，以实物、模型、影视和场景再现等方式相结合，用真实的文物，讲述这艘传奇巨轮的真实故事。

配合"泰坦尼克文物精品展"，汉古艺术馆和普利尔展览公司共同编写了《永恒的泰坦尼克——来自深海的真实故事》一书，从"造船与启航""船上生活""冰山和救援""海底发现"和"纪念"等方面，全面、多维、系统地讲述了这件悲惨海难的时代背景、具体经过和人物故事。我们从打捞出水的5000多件泰坦尼克文物中甄选出100多件套精品收入到图书中，小到一个精致的发卡，大到船体构建部分，每一件物品都是一个真实情景的再现。

这艘被号称为"永不沉没"的泰坦尼克号的沉没令人惋惜，但沉没的是巨轮，永不沉没的是泰坦尼克精神。直到今天，人们还在惊叹，泰坦尼克号上的贵族、平民、夫妻、乐手和船员，在面对汹涌冰冷的海水，面对突然而至的死亡，怎么能有那么巨大的勇气，坚守职责，不奔不逃，淡定自若，生死相依；怎么能有那么多高尚的情操，把救生艇让给孩子和妇女，把死难留给自己。这艘船几乎集结了当时世界上最著名、数量最多的亿万富翁，但他们都坚持"妇孺优先"，拒绝登救生艇；许多妻子坚定地留在丈夫身边一起面对死亡；没有一位船员选择逃生，坚守在自己的岗位到最后一刻，他们大部分人随巨轮沉入深海；即使三等舱的乘客，也大多数在最后一刻把生存的机会让给了别人。这种大爱和责任就是一种精神。

普利尔展览公司以极大的勇气冒着生命危险从海底深处的打捞、科学家对出水文物的修复保护，使泰坦尼克再现，在汉古艺术馆的接引下荡起一片浪花。若这样的接力得以传递，泰坦尼克号怎会沉没？它在人们心中永不沉没。伟大的泰坦尼克精神是人类崇高精神的集中呈现，它应该有这样一个载体予以呈现，让全球的人们都可以近距离感知与触摸，并且代代相传！

感谢美国普利尔展览公司与汉古艺术馆鼎力合作！

感谢为"泰坦尼克文物精品展"和这本图书付出心血的人们！

连 红

2018年3月于武汉光谷

POSTSCRIPT

TTitanic sinking is a big event in human history. Titanic contains various magic elements hence it is endowed with innumerable cultural symbols. Novels, documentaries and films about Titanic spring up one after another, which makes this great historical event in western culture become a widely known but ever new topic. In 1997, James Cameron, Hollywood director, presented this phase of history veritably in the form of film to people. Global audiences are moved by this film Titanic. Since the film Titanic has been released, it became popular worldwide. One of these important reasons is that this film re-produces human civilization vividly at that time. The majority of people has new understandings and attentions on Titanic via the film in China. Titanic is not simply limited to a story and itself covers various aspects such as politic, economy, culture, social life and industrial production in Europe and America societies. The influence is unbelievable from individual perspective.

In the early morning of 15th February, 1912, Titanic sank into the sea bed which is 3,800 meters deep from the sea level in the North Atlantic Ocean. The shipwreck was successfully isolated in 1985. American Premier Exhibitions, Inc. has took full responsibility for salvage, maintenance and research work of Titanic since 1987. Hangu Art Gallery brings in Titanic Antique Exhibition of American Premier Exhibitions, Inc. and exhibits about 300 items of elaborate antiques from the shipwrecks in the deep sea to present real mark at that time for visitors. The host also spends heavily on scenario restoration of this luxury and giant ship, such as captain's cabin, first class cabin, luxury grand staircase, coffee bar, promenade and boiler room. All of these provide an opportunity for visitors to be personally into the scene to go on board in Titanic. We narrate stories of this magic and great ship with real antiques from special perspectives and language of art gallery by combining real objects, models, videos and scenarios.

Hangu Art Gallery Co., Ltd. and Premier Exhibitions, Inc. co-compiles a book named A real story from deep sea -- Eternal Titanic to add luster to Titanic antique exhibition. This book introduces background information, concrete process and personage stories of this tragic shipwreck comprehensively and systematically from the aspect of building and launching, life on ship, iceberg and rescue, discovery at sea bed and memory in multiple dimensions. We select about 100 items of elaborate works from 5000 items salvaged from the deep sea and then compile this book which contains context as small as a dedicated hair pin to as large as a construction part of the ship hull. Each item is a reproduction of real scenario.

The sinking of Titanic which is called unsinkable is so unfortunate. Although Titanic sank, the Titanic spirit is unsinkable. Until today, people are still amazed at why these nobles, civilians, couples, musicians and sailors were very courageous to fulfill their duties, calm and stick together with each other in life and death and never escaped with their lives in desperate hurry, and why so many people in noble humanitarian sentiments gave up the opportunity to take the lifeboat and gave those to children and women and left death to themselves. Most celebrities and many millionaires at that time were in this ship and they insisted that children and women should be first served and refused to go on aboard lifeboats. Many wives chose to stay resolutely with their husbands to face death. No seamen chose to flee for their lives and they all stuck to their posts until the last minute. The majority of them sank into sea with Titanic. As for those passengers who were in the third-class cabin, they gave the chance of survival to others at the last minute. It is the benevolence and responsibility that is a spirit.

Staffs in Premier Exhibitions, Inc. risk their lives with great courage to salvage from deep sea. Scientists restore and protect these antiques for the Titanic reappearance. Hangu Art Gallery, as a relaying role, will make a splash. Why Titanic can sink if these exhibitions will continue? Titanic will be forever unsinkable in people's heart. The great Titanic spirit is a central presentation of lofty human spirit and it should have a carrier to present and let people worldwide know and perceive in a close distance and pass this spirit to generations.

Thanks for strong collaboration between American Premier Exhibitions, Inc. and Hangu Art Gallery.

Thanks for those who devoted to Titanic antique exhibition and this book!

Lian Hong
March 2018 at Optical Valley, Wuhan

泰坦尼克文物精品展

策 划	谢小青　　鲍道平
项目主持	连 红　　Sherry Li
形式设计	Michael Ray Pritchett
宣传推广	齐书伟　　白 京　　刘 阳　　徐 俊
	徐 婧　　程尹宣
文创开发	连 红　　陈文婷　　Ozgur Ar
筹展小组	张贝贝　　谢晓溪　　齐书伟　　陈文婷
	黎 领　　曾文强
	Adam W. Englin　　Fiona He　　Ivy Li　　Kelly Yu
	Lisha Zhang　　Raymond Poon　　Sherry Li
文物鉴定	Alexandra Klingelhofer
文物提供	RMS *Titanic*, Inc.

图录出版

主 编	谢小青　　鲍道平
副主编	连 红
编 辑	Alexandra Klingelhofer
文物摄影	Laura Pasch　　Ozgur Ar
摄影指导	Alexandra Klingelhofer
封面设计	肖 墨
版式设计	肖 墨
美国普利尔展览有限公司特邀顾问	丁 果

TITANIC THE ARTIFACT EXHIBITION

Chief Planner	Xie Xiaoqing Bao Daoping
Curator	Lian Hong Sherry Li
Designer	Michael Ray Pritchett
Promotion	Qi Shuwei Bai Jing Liu Yang Xu Jun
	Xu Jing Cheng Yinxuan
Merchandise	Lian Hong Chen Wenting Ozgur Ar
Preparation Team	Zhang Beibei Xie Xiaoxi Qi Shuwei Chen Wenting
	Li Ling Zeng Wenqiang
	Adam W. Englin Fiona He Ivy Li Kelly Yu
	Lisha Zhang Raymond Poon Sherry Li
Artifact Evaluator	Alexandra Klingelhofer
Artifact Provider	RMS *Titanic*, Inc.

CATALOG PRODUCTION

Chief Editor	Xie Xiaoqing Bao Daoping
Deputy Chief Editor	Lian Hong
Editors	Alexandra Klingelhofer
Artifact Photographer	Laura Pasch Ozgur Ar
Director of Artifact Photography	Alexandra Klingelhofer
Cover design	Xiao Mo
Layout design	Xiao Mo
Special Adviser of Premier Exhibitions, Inc.	Ding Guo

图书在版编目（CIP）数据

永恒的泰坦尼克：来自深海的真实讲述 / 汉古艺术馆，美国普利尔展览公司编. -- 武汉：湖北美术出版社，2018.3
ISBN 978-7-5394-9560-6

Ⅰ. ①永…
Ⅱ. ①汉… ②美…
Ⅲ. ①文物—世界—图集
Ⅳ. ① K86-64

中国版本图书馆 CIP 数据核字 (2018) 第 069319 号

责任编辑：陈　菊
技术编辑：范　晶
整体设计：肖　墨

永恒的泰坦尼克：来自深海的真实讲述

出版发行：	长江出版传媒　湖北美术出版社
地　　址：	武汉市洪山区雄楚大街 268 号 湖北出版文化城 B 座
电　　话：	(027) 87679985
邮政编码：	430070
印　　刷：	武汉市金港彩印有限公司
开　　本：	889mm×1194mm　1/16
印　　张：	14.5
印　　数：	10000 册
版　　次：	2018 年 3 月第 1 版 2018 年 3 月第 1 次印刷
定　　价：	310.00 元